SCHOOLDAY DIALOGUES

SCHOOLDAY DIALOGUES

A COLLECTION OF ORIGINAL DIALOGUES AND
TABLEAUX DESIGNED FOR SCHOOL EXHIBITIONS,
LITERARY SOCIETIES, AND PARLOR ENTERTAINMENTS

Compiled by

Alexander Clark

Granger Index Reprint Series

90-1869

 BOOKS FOR LIBRARIES PRESS
FREEPORT, NEW YORK

First Published 1897
Reprinted 1969

STANDARD BOOK NUMBER:
8369-6100-5

LIBRARY OF CONGRESS CATALOG CARD NUMBER:
72-103085

PREFACE.

Out of several hundred manuscript Dialogues, written in response to a liberal proposition made by the Publishers, we have chosen for publication about one-sixth, taking the editorial liberty of condensing, changing, or otherwise modifying here and there, such as are now presented in this volume. We have sought to furnish as great a variety in sentiment and style as possible, always keeping in view the fact that Dialogues, to be interesting and profitable, must be *acted* as well as uttered.

Since this work first appeared, we have made several revisions of the original matter, substituting from time to time fresh and timely Dialogues for those which seemed to have grown out of date, and in the present edition have increased the size of the volume by the addition of some twenty pages of entirely new pieces.

PREFACE.

There is no species of recitation in which young people take more delight, or evince more enthusiasm, than Declamation or Dialogue; and with a judicious selection of subject, and a natural manner of representation by voice and gesture, there is no better medium of cultivating a beautiful and effective style of elocution. It s impossible to teach reading successfully, and to excite an ambition in the breast of the pupil in this rare and pleasing accomplishment, without using lessons that call out the natural, conversational tones, the phraseology of every-day life, the vim and voice of repartee in play, in work, in trade, in the most common happenings of home, or school, or journey, or occasion whatsoever. In a Dialogue, a youngster needs no stilts on which to stretch himself and stalk forward on the high, dead level of language above his years. Here he feels his words, and enjoys their utterance as his own. Here he naturally uses the proper tone, inflection, and modulation, and, without knowing it as a rule, glides into the grace of delivery because he watches the immediate effect and listens to the consequent responses of the words he utters and means. The vocabulary of these Dialogues is not beyond the daily scenes and sounds and sentiments of Schooldays.

Although this Book is composed for the most part of carefully written and substantial subject-matter, we have admitted quite a number of humorous and amusing pieces. The proportion of the latter may be greater than will be approved by certain melancholy religionists who would infuse their moan into the very babblings of the brook and laughters of the breeze. But we have not so far out-grown our own childhood as to depreciate the joys of innocent mirth, or to say that the *only* method of correcting bad habits, of language or of life, is to frown upon them, or pretend not to see them, or dolefully to sigh and sorrow over them as misfortunes of the fall, and endure them under the name of crosses. Such a self-inflicted penance is more heterodox, in our humble judgment, than any creed, which, gospel-like, aims to correct these every-day errors of the people. Sometimes, indeed, a bit of ridicule, if ingeniously rendered, is more effectual in destroying an evil of temper or of tongue than would be a hundred homiletic discourses on human depravity, or a temple echoed full of daily prayers that word themselves in the phrases of pharisaism. We anticipate the criticisms of the would-be models of propriety—the be-solemn bachelorhood of literature—and willingly bargain for all their censures by giving in exchange our commiseration. It is an old saying that "the true orator must know how to excite the *mirth*, as well as how to command the *tears* of his audience." If the children shall enjoy this book, and are thereby aided in discovering wrong habits or dangerous tendencies in themselves or others, and are in any degree stimulated to better manners and happier life, by reading and acting these Dialogues, our object will have been more than accomplished, and our time and care more than rewarded.

PREFACE.

The art of feeling, and of teaching others how to feel the force of language, is most readily acquired from the speaking of Dialogues. There is a captivation about an exercise that requires a fellow-actor which enlists the best attention, not only of the performers themselves, but also of the auditors. The speaker realizes that he is to impress his hearers as much by the manner as by the matter of his discourse. Mere routine reading, paragraph by paragraph, in parrot-like regularity of sound, as a task to be told, will become as monotonous as a bell that is *tolled*.

It is said of a prosy minister, that, while, on a certain occasion, he was reading to his congregation a chapter from the Bible, he put several of his hearers to sleep. His voice was keyed to a meaningless mono tone, and his whole manner was as spiritless and as senseless as the muttering of a mill. For some ministers do *go*, as machines, by some sort of fuel-fed force, rather than by the vital impulses of head and heart, as men. So went he, and as an inevitable consequence, he rumbled the people off into the land of dreams. Then, looking up from his book, and seeing his hearers soothed under his voice like babes by mothers' lullabies, he became indignant at their stupidity, and wishing to make a direct impression, his feeling took action, and he seized the Bible with both hands and hurled it at their heedless heads, saying, in a far more natural and honest manner than that in which he had been reading, "If you will not *hear* the truth, you miserable sinners.

I am determined to make you *feel* it." That minister never delivered a more eloquent passage in his life. He felt what he said if he did not feel what he was reading, and he made the people feel just what he felt himself, and perhaps some of them a little more! He was roused and in earnest; then tone, emphasis, and modulation, and gesture were natural. He did a foolish thing; but he did it in a forcible and striking manner.

We have sometimes thought that many clergymen, teachers, and parents will have a fearful account to render for the indifference with which they read the Scriptures. What beauties, sympathies, grandeurs, and glories are perverted and mutilated by the task-readers of the Sacred Word! The devil could not more effectually burlesque religion than to employ certain dyspeptic professors of it, to go about reading the Bible! Eyes have they, but they see not. Tongues have they, but they talk not. Hearts have they, but they feel not. They repulse the smiling children by their funereal solemnities when nobody has died!

Not long since we heard the eightieth Psalm read with such a cog-wheel coarseness and clatter of expression that the beautiful petition, "Turn us again," sounded as though it would all be chipped to pieces in the machinist's lathe. Frequently on funeral occasions, in our hearing, has the fifteenth chapter of the First Epistle to the Corinthians been so attacked, so wounded, so slain, so utterly buried by professional friends to its glorious truth, that it really seemed to us that there would be no resurrection for ever! When will teachers and preachers use the means that are natural, accessible, and efficient, in training the young to read as they talk? We verily believe that many of the sectarianisms of the religious world, arise from an ignorance of the rules of emphasis in reading the Bible, rather than from an istinct meanings of the truth upon the Blessed Pages

An intelligent young Christian student was noticed to come into chapel service every day regularly after the Scripture lesson and singing were finished. The Professor called him to an account for his delinquency, and he excused himself on the ground of very tender 'eelings, not being able to endure the butchery of hymn and Scripture. Said he: "My mother used to *read* the Bible to me, and I can't associate those hallowed memories with the heartless roughness I must hear in this chapel. *I can't do it.*" He was excused, and the pulpit readings were improved thereafter.

The subject of reading, or elocution, should occupy, not more time, more attention. The young should e taught to read as they talk, freely, feelingly, with the spirit, with the understanding, with all the emphasis and action of graceful gesture. Enthusiasm must be excited, in some way, ambition aroused, and the natural voice called out as a response to the questionings of common sense.

If these Schoolday Dialogues shall be properly studied, their lessons fully understood, and their spirit fully realized, their delivery will be, we trust, so acceptable and so impressive, that our well-intended labors may not have been in vain.

ALEXANDER CLARK

CONTENTS.

TRUE MANLINESS	M. L. R.	15
THE TOBACCO PLEDGE	Elizabeth E. Ralston.	30
THE NEW MUFF AND COLLAR	Kate E. Peet.	34
CHOOSE YOUR WORDS	Barbara Broome.	38
EFFECTS OF WAR	Ceria.	44
THE TWO INTERPRETERS OF DREAMS	Hattie Herbert.	49
THE FOUR SEASONS	Louise E. V. Boyd.	54
SCHOOL AFFAIRS IN RIVERHEAD DISTRICT	C. W. Deans.	58
NOVEL READING		67
THE DEMONS OF THE GLASS	Oliver Optic.	70
THE TWELVE MONTHS	Henry H. Johnson.	75
THE NEW PREACHER	Silonius.	78
THE SEASONS	Hattie Home.	82
LITTLE ANGELS	Emma C. Hollinger.	87
THE YOUNG STATESMAN	Beno.	92
TWO WAYS OF LIFE	H. C. H.	95
TOO GOOD TO ATTEND COMMON SCHOOL	Eliza Doolittle.	97
FIRESIDE COLLOQUY	Joseph W. Leatherman.	101
POCAHONTAS	Mary Hartwell.	106
BEAUTY OF FACE AND BEAUTY OF SOUL	Abbie J. Thornton.	109
UNCLE ZEKE'S OPINION	W. H. Sabean.	113
SPELLING CLASS	D. R. Brubaker.	120
THE TWO TEACHERS	Hattie Herbert.	124

CONTENTS

MEMORY AND HOPE	Mrs. L. E. V. Boyd.	127
A CONTENTIOUS COMMUNITY	Eureka.	132
LOST AND FOUND	Emma E. Brewster.	138
THE TRI-COLORS	Emma Fields.	142
ANNIE'S PARTY	L. A. B. C.	144
THE RECLAIMED BROTHER; OR, THE CHAIN OF ROSES.	H. E. McBride.	150
REFORMATION	H. B. Niles.	154
SEEING A GHOST	Julia A. Crouch.	158
THE MOTTO OR EXAMPLE	Mrs. C. M. Peat.	162
CHOOSING A TRADE OR PROFESSION	Geo. D. Hunt.	169
CHILD-PHILOSOPHY	H. A. Duncan.	174
THE NOBLEST HERO	Alice Gray.	176
WOMAN'S RIGHTS	Emma Zeliff.	179
THE ORPHAN'S TRUST	H. C. Hunt.	186

SCHOOLDAY DIALOGUES.

TRUE MANLINESS.

CHARACTERS.

MR. HOWARD, a wealthy gentleman.
MR. WAYNE, teacher.
TOM JONES, a blusterer.
CALEB NOTT, a toady.
CHARLES STEPHENS, son of a poor widow. } Pupils.
HARRY DARE.
EDWARD BURTON.

ACT I. SCENE 1.—*The School Room.*

TEACHER.—Boys, I have something to tell you after school, or rather, you must be prepared to hear something. I believe, however, that I had better not tell it.

BOYS.—Oh, please, teacher, do tell us. What is it?

TEACHER.—No, I shall not tell you; but you shall hear it this afternoon, nevertheless. Now attend to your studies. [*Goes on correcting exercises.*]

TOM JONES [*to Caleb*].—What a mum fellow our teacher is, to be sure; isn't he?

CALEB.—Yes; he might as well out with it now.

TEACHER.—Attend to your studies, boys. Are you talking?

TOM.—No, teacher, only Charlie Stephens, he makes such a noise with his lips. [*Charlie looks confused, but does not speak.*]

TEACHER [*severely*].—Tom Jones, how often must I correct you in speaking? It is unnecessary to use the personal pronoun when you use the noun. A great boy like you—almost a man—should be more careful Charles Stephens, you must make less noise studying; you disturb me.

Tom *to* [*Charlie*].—I'll be even with you for that lecture; see if I don't.

CALEB.—Hide his old cap after school.

[*Enter Mr. Howard. Mr. Wayne advances, and they shake hands. Boys rise.*]

MR. HOWARD.—I am pleased, Mr. Wayne, to see your school in such good order. Have you mentioned my proposition to your pupils?

TEACHER.—I have not, sir; but merely intimated to them that they would hear *something*. I preferred leaving it to yourself. Boys, you know who this gentleman is?

BOYS [*all*].—Yes, sir; Mr. Howard.

MR. H.—Thank you, young gentlemen; I am glad you remember me. [*Boys bow.*] Your respected teacher tells me that he has prepared you to hear some particular news.

BOYS.—Yes, sir.

MR. H.—Well, I shall now proceed to tell you what it is. I am, as you may be aware, a great friend to education. [*Boys bow.*] Education, my young friends, is better than houses and lands—better than gold. But *mental* education, without *moral*, is worse than useless The boy who possesses one without the other, may be compared to a man who has eyes, yet is blind; who has ears, yet can not hear. Do you understand me?

BOYS.—Yes, sir.

MR. H.—Very well. Now, that you may learn to appreciate the value of moral education, I have determined to offer a gold eagle to that boy whose meritorious conduct best deserves a reward.

BOYS.—Oh, thank you, sir; you are very kind.

MR. H.—Remember, boys, that you all can not get it but the *trying* for it will be an advantage in many ways. First, striving for this prize will beget in you a noble emulation. Secondly, you will, if you *really* desire to obtain it, practice many virtues—patience, self-denial, energy, etc. Thirdly, you will, in the pursuit of this prize, acquire a habit of perseverance, which alone will

SCHOOLDAY DIALOGUES. 17

oe worth many half eagles to you. Fourthly—I believe I have no fourthly, except to say, that your term of proration will expire in one month from to-day—when I shall have the pleasure of bestowing a reward on the most deserving, amid, I trust, the approving smiles of his noble-minded companions. Good afternoon, young gentlemen; good afternoon, Mr. Wayne. [*Exit.*]

BOYS [*all together*].—Who'll get it, I wonder? I mean to try. I don't; 'twould be no use. Ten dollars in gold—I wish I had it—etc.

TEACHER.—Boys; silence! Is this rude clamor the beginning of your competition for a reward of merit? Now act more like the gentlemen Mr. Howard calls you. As it wants but twenty minutes until the hour of dismissal, I shall let you off now. But tell me, who intends to gain the prize? Tom Jones, do you?

TOM.—No, sir; I couldn't get it if I did try; and, besides, old Howard is rich enough to have offered twenty dollars, and I call him *stingy*.

BOYS.—Oh, shame! he had no need to give it at all.

TEACHER.—Thomas, I am astonished to hear you speak in such a disrespectful manner; but I hope you are not in earnest. Ned Burton, will you try?

NED.—Yes, sir; and I'll get it, too.

TEACHER.—Indeed; how do you know?

NED.—Why, I never tried for any thing I didn't get.

TOM.—You didn't get the book that master offered for that problem in algebra, and you tried for it.

NED [*aside*].—I'll get satisfaction out of you, though; see if I don't.

TOM [*sneeringly*].—Well, maybe you'll get satisfaction; but you wont get the ten dollars.

TEACHER.—Charlie Stephens, will you get it, too?

CHARLIE.—Oh! if I only could.

TEACHER.—Why, what would you do with it?

TOM [*aside*].—Buy a little doll-baby.

TEACHER.—Answer, Charles; what would you do?

[*Charles endeavors to speak, but falters, and turns away. Tom—behind teacher—places one arm across the other, pretending to dandle a baby; sings softly, By-o-baby; buy a dolly with ten dollars. Boys laugh.*]

TEACHER [*musingly*].—I can not understand Charles Stephens. I would fancy he had some trouble if he were not too young. It must be only silly bashfulness, and I must cure him of it. Boys, what are you laughing at?

CALEB.—Why, sir, Charlie looks so funny when he's crying; just like a girl.

TEACHER [*sternly*].—I do not see why a girl should ook more funny than a boy. Charles, are you crying?

CHARLIE.—No, sir; I am not crying.

TOM.—Only mighty near it.

TEACHER.—Tom, I insist on your being silent, or, at least, you must cease these personal remarks. Because you have sense enough to be neither bashful nor vainglorious [*looks at Charlie and Ned*], you should not tease those who are either. Now you can leave, boys; and I wish you, *each and all*, to try for Mr. Howard's prize; for if he be really pleased with you, his generosity will not be limited to this act; but I must not tell any more. However, I hope you will all deserve it, though only one can get it. [*Exeunt omnes.*]

SCENE 2. *Immediately after* SCENE 1.—*Boys at Play.*

TOM JONES.—I wonder now who will get that ten dollars. I call it a mean trick not to give twenty. The old miser could afford it just as easy, and then 'twould be worth having, though not worth trying for, I say.

CALEB.—No, not worth trying for, I say, too; but, Tom, you could get it, couldn't you? Ten dollars arn't picked up in the street.

TOM.—Why couldn't *you* get it, if you are so anxious for it?

CALEB.—Oh, Tom, 'twouldn't be any use for *me* to try Old master doesn't think that much of me; but *you* could wheedle it out of his own pocket, if 'twas only in, you're uch a pet of his.

TOM.—No I aint, though.

CALEB.—Why, didn't you hear what he said to you when that cry-baby, Charlie, began to blubber?

TOM.—Oh, you want to gammon me now. I'm not

SCHOOLDAY DIALOGUES. 19

quite *that* green, though. Here comes Burton; now I'll teach him to brag.

CALEB.—Now don't, Tom; master would be sure to hear of it. See what he says first.

NED.—I say, Tom, let's have a game of foot-ball.

TOM [*aside*].—To be sure! *he's* trying for it in earnest [*Aloud.*] How about that satisfaction, Ned?

NED.—Oh, hang the satisfaction [*aside*] till I get th prize.

TOM.—Well, I'll hang it, if you like. I see you're going in to win.

NED [*indifferently.*]—No; I needn't try. There's so many better fellows in the school than I am. Besides, my father's rich, and I can get ten dollars any time I want it.

TOM.—You *think* you can!

CALEB [*sidling up to Ned*].—Ned, I think you've about the smartest chance going. I'll tell master how you forgave Tom, after all his meanness, and 'twill stand in your favor.

NED.—Oh, go 'way. I don't want to have any thing to say to you.

CALEB [*bitterly*].—You don't, don't you? Well, maybe you'll come down yet, Ned Burton, for all you hold yourself so high. [*Goes off by himself.*]

NED.—Where's that little girl, Charlie? I guess *he'll* get it; *he* never does any thing wrong; oh, no, not he!

TOM.—I say, now, that's too bad. If a cry-baby, girl-boy, like Charlie Stephens, gets it, I'll leave school.

SEVERAL BOYS.—So will I. So will I.

HARRY D.—And why may not Charlie get it, as well as any one else, if he deserves it; and he wont get it unless he does deserve it.

BOYS.—Oh, preacher! preacher!

TOM.—Maybe *you'll* get it, you think?

HARRY.—No, I'll not get it; for I couldn't be the best; but I'm above joining in against a fellow that's not here to take his own part, and who is the best of us, anyway.

TOM.—Come now, Harry Dare, I like that; maybe, since you're so ready to talk for the "one that's the best amongst us," you'll be willing to fight for him, too. You'll not say he would do *that* for himself, I guess.

HARRY.—Yes, I'll fight for him as long as you please; and I am a match for you, too, Tom Jones, big as you are [*Puts himself in an attitude.*]

NED [*hastily*].—Oh, come now, boys, don't make fools of yourselves, fighting about a fellow who hasn't spirit enough to open his mouth.

TOM.—Well, I do not care about fighting, particularly; let's shake hands, Hal [*aside*]; Ned's bound to win; how disappointed he is that we don't fight. I hate a hypocrite.

CALEB [*approaching hastily*].—I say, boys; oh, what I have to tell you!

ALL.—What? what?

CALEB.—Let me get breath—I shall die laughing. You know our girl?

BOYS.—No; we don't know your girl. What about her?

CALEB.—You don't understand me. I mean the one that goes to our school—Charlie Stephens.

ALL.—Yes, yes; go on.

CALEB.—Well, while you were talking, I saw him scuddin' across the field at a two-forty pace; so, thinks I, I'll see what *you're* up to. So I follows him a safe distance, or he'd a heard me.

HARRY D.—Mean spy!

CALEB.—So, on I sneaks after him, slowly, slowly, till he came to that little, rickety, tumble-down hole of a hut, at the edge of the woods. So in there my gentleman goes. You know, none of us never could find out where he put up. So, my fine boy goes in; and I sees a hole of a window at one side, so up I goes, giving him time to get seated to his piano, as I supposed, from his high and mighty airs. In I peeps, and there—oh, my, I can't tell you [*laughing immoderately*].

BOYS.—Come, tell us, Cale; go ahead with it.

CALEB.—It's too good; I can't tell you.

TOM.—You'd better, or I'll shake it out of you.

HARRY D.—I'd like to shake his mean soul out of him.

CALEB.—Well, here goes. Oh, gracious! I peeped

SCHOOLDAY DIALOGUES.   21

n at the window, and there was king Charlie, with—what do you think?

ALL.—What? tell us what?

CALEB.—With—oh, my! with a *great, big, blue check woman's apron on.*

ALL.—Hurrah for Miss Charlie; hurrah for the boy with a blue check woman's apron on. Go on, go on, Cale.

CALEB.—Yes; oh, I'll die with laughter. I most burst, trying to keep in there.

BOYS [*impatiently*].—Well; what was he doing?

CALEB.—I'm coming to it. What do you think —*washing the dishes!*

BOYS.—Hurrah for the dish-washer!

ONE.—I'll tell my mother to hire him—she wants a gal.

ANOTHER.—I'll hire him myself. I'm going to housekeeping.

TOM.—Now, Harry, what do you say for your paragon? I believe that's the word; aint it?

HARRY [*aside; angrily*].—I did not think he was such a milksop. I'll let him go. [*Aloud*]: why, perhaps, it wasn't him at all.

BOYS.—Oh, now, that wont go down; you know it was; but go on, Caleb—tell us the rest; did he wash them clean?

CALEB.—It was the poorest kind of a place, I tell you. He was a standing at a little table, where he couldn't see me; but I could see him. He was a washing away, and I heard something else—a woman—talking. Charlie was saying: "Mother, don't you be tiring yourself washing little Alice; when I'm done the pots, and pails, and kettles, I'll wash her, too; just you lean back in your chair and rest;" and then the woman says: "No, Charlie, this doesn't tire me; and you have your lessons to study, too, for you know I want you to keep your place." Now, wasn't that mean—just putting him up to keeping us out of our places?

TOM.—I say, boys, let's go, after school to-morrow, and see Charlie washin' dishes. Say, shall we?

BOYS.—Yes, yes; let's go.

HARRY.—I, for one, will not go. I'm no eavesdropper nor spy.

CALEB.—Do you mean to say I am?

HARRY.—Yes.

[*Caleb slinks away. Approaches Tom, and in dumb show, asks him to fight Harry.*]

TOM.—No, no; fight your own battles. I've enough for me. Come, boys, let's go home, and dream we've nabbed old Howard, and each got a ten dollar gold piece. [*Exeunt.*]

NED.—I'll go along to keep them in order; 'twill go hard with me, but I will win this reward; pshaw, this ten dollars, I mean. With it, I can reach the city at last, and then good-bye to being a good boy. [*Exit slowly.*]

End of first Act.

ACT II. SCENE 1.—*Charlie sitting on a log at the edge of the woods, in a desponding attitude.*

CHARLES.—No, I can not endure it any longer. I *will* leave school, though to do so, will be to give up all my bright dreams, all my cherished hopes; for, poor boy though I am, I *have* dreams and hopes. Yes, I have dreamed of a time when I could support my dear mother and my little sister. [*Here Mr. Howard and Mr. Wayne approach, unperceived; they see Charlie, and stop Charlie continues.*] When the education she has worked so hard to give me, might be made the medium and the evidence of my gratitude to her. I *have* hoped, but it is no use. For three weeks, my schoolmates have taunted and jeered me. Some way they have found out how I work, and every moment they can, they taunt me by saying, "Polly, put the kettle on," or ask me if my dishcloth is clean, and the baby's face washed? Oh! if one of them had a sick mother, who still sewed day after day, and far into the night, how gladly I would help him with the work he did to help her. I would not call him a girl-boy nor tantalize him; but I must give it up. Mr. Ross will give me three dollars a week to mind his store, and I must take it. If I could only get that ten dollars, it would enable mother to take a rest, and then she would get well; but I need not think of it; they are all against me, even Mr. Wayne. [*Rises, and exit slowly. Mr. Howard and Mr. Wayne look at each other.*]

MR. H.—Is that boy one of your pupils, Mr. Wayne*

MR. W.—He is, and he seems in great trouble.

MR. H.—Yes, but it is such as can be easily remedied I hope. What is it?

MR. W.—Well, really, Mr. Howard, I am half ashamed to say that I do not know. Charles Stephens has always been so reserved that I could not understand him, and I dislike any thing like secretiveness above all. I can forgive what to others might seem graver faults, if accompanied by an upright spirit. There's Tom Jones, for example; he is heedless, often displays a spirit of rebellion, but still, he is so candid——

MR. H. [*interrupting*].—Excuse me, my dear sir, but I do not think that Tom Jones' candor, which may really be only a spirit of bravado, should extenuate the commission of the faults you mention. I happen to know something about him myself. As for this other boy, what faults do you find in him beside the reserve you so dislike?

MR. W.—I must say I can not find any fault with him except on that score—he is quiet, obedient, and studious.

MR. H. [*warmly*].—My dear sir, what more would you have? We must not look for perfection in a school boy. I shall be satisfied with a *very good one*, for whose benefit I can expend a portion of my superfluous wealth. If I find such a one, I shall, as you know, aid him to prosecute his studies, enable him to enter college, give him a trade or profession, or the means of starting in business, as he may prefer, and if he prove worthy, be a friend to him for life. I am not an advocate for posthumous charities. The good I do now may be indefinitely multiplied if *my* boy, when he grows up, should do the same for another, and he for a third, and so on.

MR. W —Yes, I see; like Benjamin Franklin and his dollar, you would extend the sphere of your benevolence beyond your own time.

MR. H.—I don't call it benevolence. I have more money than I need, or shall ever use, and I was once a poor struggling boy myself, who would have given ten years of his life for this chance that I offer, of an education.

MR. W.—Well, Mr. Howard, I wish to assist you conscientiously, therefore, I shall try and find out the secret of Charlie's reserve, and give him an equal chance with the rest, of profiting by your liberality.

MR. H.—Do not misunderstand me; it is the most meritorious who is to gain the reward, both the present slight one, and the future more valuable one, whether it be Tom Jones or Charles Stephens. But I would like you to find out the cause of his trouble, and let me know.

MR. W.—I shall not fail to do so. [*Exeunt.*]

SCENE 2.—*The school-room. Boys standing around teacher.*

TEACHER.—Well, boys, the day after will be *the* day Already I have seen the truth of Mr. Howard's assertion that though *all* can not gain the prize he has offered, yet all would be the better for trying. I think you have all been trying, for there is certainly the evidence of it in the increased subordination, and diligence of the greater number of you, at least.

NED B.—Well, teacher, I don't care so much for the prize, for, as you know, my father is very rich; but I would like to please you and Mr. Howard, who is so kind.

HARRY D.—The hypocrite!

TEACHER.—What did you mutter, Harry Dare? Don't hesitate so; answer me.

NED.—Please, teacher, don't mind making him answer

TEACHER.—Why not?

NED.—I don't want him to be punished—or I don't mean that; but I do not care what is said of me, if I only have your approbation and that of my conscience

HARRY.—Now I *will* speak; I said——

TEACHER.—Harry, be silent. Ned Burton, I should be sorry to think you did not merit the approval you speak of; but your words are almost *too* fair and good Take care that your actions correspond with them.

HARRY.—Master, I *will* speak, at the risk of your displeasure. I said Ned Burton was a hypocrite, and I maintain it.

TEACHER.—Can you prove what you assert?

NED.—No, sir, he can't; he's no witnesses.

HARRY [*indignantly*].—Witnesses! my word is as good as yours.

TEACHER.—Well, say what you have to say.

HARRY.—Yesterday you blamed Charlie Stephens for not having written his Latin exercise, and when he said he had written it, but could not find it, you would scarcely believe it.

TEACHER.—Yes, I remember; go on. [*Ned appears agitated, but says nothing.*]

HARRY.—At noon, to-day, I wished to get something from my portfolio. Ned Burton has one exactly like mine. I went to my desk, and to my surprise saw the portfolio *on*, instead of *inside* the desk. I opened it, and the first paper I saw was Charlie Stephens' exercise. Surprised at this, I turned over another leaf, when I saw at once the portfolio was not mine. I looked for the name, and found it to be Edward Burton. He has known of the exercise being there, for I have seen him looking all through his portfolio since then.

TEACHER.—Edward, what have you to say to this charge?

NED.—Nothing, sir, except that it is false.

HARRY.—Look in his portfolio.

NED.—Yes, as you did, sneaking Paul Pry!

HARRY.—I did not pry; your portfolio was on my desk, and I thought it was mine.

NED.—Oh! yes, that's easily said.

TEACHER.—Boys, cease this crimination and recrimination. An inspection of the portfolio will settle the question. Tom, bring it to me.

NED.—No, sir, I deny your right to inspect my possessions. He shall not get it.

TEACHER.—*Shall* not! Do you say he shall not obey my commands?

NED.—Yes, sir, I say he shall not touch my property

TEACHER.—Tom, bring me his portfolio.

[*Ned makes an effort to get it, but is held by several boys. Then assumes a defiant expression.*]

TOM.—Here, sir.

[*Teacher looks through the portfolio, and draws forth the lost exercise. Boys utter various sounds of astonishment and horror.*]

TEACHER [*sternly*].—Edward Burton, I am shocked and pained beyond expression, to find that one of my boys—one, too, whom I trusted, and who but to-day made professions so greatly at variance with such conduct—should be guilty of the great wrong of wilfully seeking to injure another, and adding to that wrong the grievous one of falsehood. You are dismissed from this school, and sorry I am to be compelled to say, that in your case there are no extenuating circumstances. In order to lessen the chance of another gaining an offered reward, you hesitate not to subject him to unjust censure, nor to expose him to the suspicion of falsehood. Charles, I regret my hasty action toward you; as for you, Edward, you are no longer a pupil of mine, but if, after long reflection on your wicked conduct——

NED [*interrupting*].—Oh, if you mean I'll want to come back, and beg pardon, and all that, you're very much mistaken, and as for your dismissal, why if I had only succeeded in getting old Howard's ten dollars, I intended to dismiss myself right off, for I am sick of this low school, where rowdies and dishwashers get all the favors. You wanted to find me out a villain, and now pretend to be sorry that your scheme was successful.

TEACHER.—Take your books, and depart; I will hear no more.

[*Ned collects books, etc., goes to the door, stops, and with an ironical bow, says:*]

NED.—Good-by, sir; I wish you joy of your *excellent* scholars and your liberal friends. [*Exit.*]

SCENE 3. *School Room. Mr. Howard and Mr. Wayne seated.*

MR. H.—Well, sir, his mother, you say, appears to be delicate?

TEACHER.—Yes, sir; it is my honest opinion that one year more of her present existence would terminate it.

MR. H.—And she says that, but for this son, she could not manage to get along?

TEACHER.—Yes; Charles has, when freed from his school duties, earned, on an average, from one to two dollars a week by doing various little services for th farmers living about here, particularly, carrying mes sages, an office in which he is invaluable; they say, he never makes a mistake, never requires to be told twice, and is always punctual and prompt.

MR. H.—I think more of his assisting his mother in her housework, for that shows a spirit which is above false pride, a quality I detest. So many boys are ruined by the pernicious idea that it is degrading to do aught that seems, to their perverted view, *unwomanly*. A want of manliness is degrading; but few of the young understand that true manliness consists in *doing our duty*, whatever it may be, unmoved by the sneers of others. But, I say, Mr. Wayne, I am a pretty good judge of human nature, or boy nature, am I not?

MR. W.—I must say, you are, sir. Your penetration in this case was greater than mine.

MR. H.—Ah, ha! I thought you would agree to that Well, time is nearly up; and now be sure to tell th boys every thing; that is, tell them all about Charlie's devotion to his mother; but do not, of course, say any thing of my intention to provide for his mother and sister until he is able to do so himself.

MR. W.—I shall attend to it, sir.

[*Enter boys. They bow to Mr. Howard and teacher and stand in order.*]

TEACHER.—Well, boys, this afternoon will decide which of you will obtain the reward offered for good conduct by your kind friend, Mr. Howard; a reward, which, as I intimated, will not stop at the sum of money offered to-day. Take your seats.

MR. H.—No, young gentlemen, the one who is proved most worthy shall receive substantial and lasting evidence of my good-will. Your teacher tells me that you have, with one exception, appeared actuated by a desire to improve. I trust this improvement will continue, and I shall feel a pride and pleasure in continuing the warm friend to education, as manifested in this school, that I always have been. Mr. Wayne, will you proceed?

TEACHER —As Mr. Howard has said, I have been pleased to see a decided improvement in many of you, and all of you have merited in different degrees. I have, owever, already decided upon the one, who, judged by his actions in school and out of it, has best deserved the prize. [*Sensation among the boys.*] But, before announcing his name, I shall first tell you a little story. Not very far from your school house there is a little cottage, in which dwell a widow and her two children. These children, the elder of whom is a boy, she has supported by the constant and untiring, though not altogether unaided labor of her hands. The aid she has had was given by her son, in the intervals of his school duties. But I should have said that this poor woman has contrived to keep her son constantly at school, hoping that the education he thus acquired would be the means of enabling him to support her when she could no longer provide for him. He assisted her in various ways, earning now and then a little money, but most of all in her *housework*. [*Boys appear surprised.*] Yes, young gentlemen, though *you* may think it derogatory to the dignity of a boy, it seems he did not. His mother, whose health was enfeebled by her efforts in behalf of her children, would have sunk long ago had not her tasks been lightened by her devoted assistant, who took upon himself the hardest, as well as the most menial, duties of the household. It is unnecessary for me to enumerate in detail all that he did. Although his schoolmates had frequently ridiculed his sensitive and retiring disposition, they went no further, until, by some unfortunate, and, I fear, underhand means, they discovered his mode of spending the hours given by them to play. From that moment there was no more peace for him At every opportunity, he was saluted by such terms as dish-washer, baby-tender, and similar ones. This became at last so unendurable that he resolved to quit the school, and take a situation in a store. Against this determination his love of knowledge and his mother's

wishes both contended, and in the end prevailed. That
you may not under-estimate the heroism of his course—
for heroism it certainly was—in thus continuing to en
dure the taunts and jeers of his school-fellows, I shall
merely say, that his sensitiveness is so great that, on
one occasion, being unjustly and harshly accused of a
fault, he was unable to defend himself, and only chance
revealed the truth. This boy, whose true manliness ena-
bled him to endure contempt and ridicule, rather than
swerve from the path of duty, is, I need scarcely add,
one of your own companions; and to him is adjudged
the prize, with, I hope, your approval.

Boys.—Yes, indeed, sir; he deserves it. We didn't
know his mother was sick, etc.

Mr. H.—Yes, young gentlemen, you truly say he deserves it; and I am glad to know, by the heartiness of
your replies, that you speak as you think. Charles
Stephens, by the decision of your teacher, and the
approval of your school-mates, you are entitled to the
prize. And while I commend your example in the past
to them, I trust that neither you nor they will ever be
led away from the right by ridicule, and *never* consider
any service that is done for a mother as detracting in
the slightest degree from your character for TRUE MAN-
LINESS. [*Curtain falls.*]

THE TOBACCO PLEDGE.

CHARACTERS.

John Lossing.
Albert Miller.
Mr. Wise, their Teacher.

Albert.—Good morning, John. Where is your craft bound for so early?

John.—Good morning. As you are trying to talk sailor style, I will try, too. My craft is steering, all sails set, for school. A delightful harbor, where all such vessels as ours may anchor in safety from the storms of temptation, sure to assail those who remain out at sea.

A.—Well done. That's first rate. But come with me to the grocery, and then I will go with you to school.

J.—Why, what do you want there?

A.—I coaxed five cents from father, last night, and I am going to have some cigars.

J.—You have never smoked any, and they will make you sick. I would rather not go.

A.—Oh, come along, and I will give you one. We will have some fun, I'll warrant.

J.—I thank you. I never use tobacco, for a number of reasons. One is, "It is a wicked waste of money." Just think: if you begin now, at eleven years, and spend five cents a day until you are twenty-one years old, to what it will amount. What a number of good books and papers it would get! $182.50; count for yourself.

A.—But every boy, who is any thing of a man, smokes, and I am as much of a man as any of them. Why, all use it when they get big, and you will, too. It is just because your mother will not let you.

J.—No, that is not the reason. But my mother has shown me that it is a sin, and a poison that will destroy my health. And I promised her I would "Touch not, taste not, handle not the unclean thing."

A.—My father uses it, and so does our minister, and nearly every body I know. And they would not use it if they thought it was a sin. Why, ministers preach against every thing that is wrong, and I have seen them chewing in church. Now, what can you say to that?

J.—They do not view the subject in the right light, or they would not do so. Mother says, the Bible forbids "Using our money for that which is not meat, or our substance for that which satisfieth not." Now if it is poison, it is not meat; it will not sustain life There fore, it is wrong.

A.—Yes, yes; that may all be if it *is* a poison; but now are you going to prove that? It has been raised for hundreds of years, and I have never seen or heard tel. of a case of poisoning from tobacco.

J.—It can be proved, both by chemistry and physiology, that it is a poison. And if no one uses enough at one time to kill him, yet the continued use will debilitate the body, and bring on diseases which do end in death.

A.—I do not know any thing about chemistry; but I would like to know a part of what you seem to know so well.

J.—Any reliable work on chemistry will tell you that by analysis a property has been discovered, called *nicotine*. This is so poisonous that one drop placed on the tongue of a cat will kill it in five minutes. Chemistry says that the effect of tobacco, in small quantities, on the human frame is of a very pleasing character for a time: the nerves are quietly lulled into a very comfortable feeling, and may for the moment endure more than they can unstimulated. But after the undue stimulus is over, they are weaker than before; and thus begins the slow but sure undermining of life.

A.—"Why, how you talk!" It all sounds very good; but I intend to ask some one else. I shall not take your word for it.

J.—I do not want you to take my word for it. But just reflect how many persons we see who are pale, and nervous, by smoking; complaining of headache, dyspepsia, weak stomach, etc. All this is caused by imposing upon the stomach with the use of tobacco.

A.—You say it makes headache; I say it cures toothache. I have seen it done more than once.

J.—Yes; it cures the toothache on the same principle

any other narcotic would. But here comes Mr. Wise, on his way to school, and we can walk along, and ask him about what I have said. He understands chemistry and physiology.

A.—Ha! ha! ha! That will not do you any good. Choose some one else.

J.—What is the matter? Why will he do me no good?

A.—See, he is smoking now. Do you expect him to take his cigar from his mouth, and say: "Yes, I am poisoning myself. I am using my money for that which is not meat. I am sinning?" Ha! ha! that is too funny.

J.—No; I do not want him to answer so; neither do I intend to ask the questions. You must do that. It would sound like impertinence from me, while you can do it with perfect propriety.

[*Mr. Wise approaches, smoking. They meet.*]

A. & J.—Good morning.

Mr. W.—Good morning, boys; I am glad to see you out so early. You were very busy talking when we met; may I know what it was about?

J.—Yes, sir; and we want you to decide which of us is right.

Mr. W.—Well, what is it? I will decide justly, to the best of my knowledge.

A.—I wanted John to go with me to get some cigars, and he tried to make me believe that it was wrong, and that any person who knew any thing about chemistry would acknowledge there was poison in tobacco.

Mr. W.—What else did he say, that you want my opinion concerning?

A.—Oh, much more. He said the Bible forbade us to use our money for that which is not meat, etc. He said, if tobacco would kill, it was not meat, and that it was wicked to waste our money so.

Mr. W.—It is true, it is wrong to spend our money needlessly. But how does he prove the rest?

A.—Let him tell it as he told it to me.

J.—The chemical analysis of tobacco has discovered a poison called *nicotine* so active that one drop placed on the tongue of a cat will produce death in five minutes

A.—Is that true? Is that true, Mr. Wise?

Mr. W.—His authority is very good. I believe that statement is correct. But, John, you do not know of any person being killed by tobacco, do you?

J.—I do not, sir. But a great many weak and sick persons complaining of headache, dyspepsia (and I know not what else), are made such by debilitating the stomach with tobacco.

Mr. W.—You said before tobacco was stimulating how then can it debilitate?

J.—The very fact that it stimulates at one time is proof of debility afterward. And you know, sir, these secretions of the glands of the mouth are absolutely necessary to assist the stomach in its office of digestion. When the saliva has become saturated with tobacco no one swallows it, but expels it; thus the stomach is deprived of this help, and becomes diseased or overworked.

A.—Well, it's not wrong for old folks to smoke. It is such a comfort when they get so old and blind they can not read to enjoy themselves.

J.—They are then only suffering from its use when young. Perhaps if they had never injured their eyes with the use of tobacco, their sight might not have failed so seriously. It has a powerful effect upon the eyes. If you were to smoke a cigar now it could be told on the eyes as easily as any other way.

A.—Why, I never heard any person talk so about tobacco in all my life. I have heard them scold about it being dirty and hateful, and all such. But is this true, Mr. Wise? If it is, I will never use it.

Mr. W.—John, you reason like a scholar. Although I use tobacco, I dare not dispute you. You have religion and science on your side. But who taught you this? You are too young to have learned yourself.

J.—My mother taught me, sir; and I promised her I would "Touch not, taste not, handle not the unclean thing."

Mr. W. [*throwing away his cigar*].—You are right, my noble boy. I have thrown away my cigar, and will sign your pledge of "total abstinence." I have reasoned and smoked against my own convictions long enough. You have a worthy mother; I wish there were more such.

J.—I signed no pledge, sir; but gave my word,

which I intend to keep as faithfully as if written on the Bible.

A.—Can't we get up a pledge? I want to sign, and get others to do so, too.

MR. W.—You draw one up and see what success you will have. Your cause is a good one.

A.—I would sir, if I could, but I can not compose it right.

MR. W.—John will help you. Here is a pencil and paper—now go to work.

[*After a short whispering, they approach with the following:*]

A.—Will this do, sir? [*Reads.*]

WHEREAS our school-mate, John Lossing, has proved to us that the use of tobacco is both morally and physically wrong, therefore, we, the undersigned

Resolve, 1st, We will "Touch not, taste not, handle not," tobacco in any shape or form.

Resolve, 2d, We will do all we can to persuade others of our friends to join us.

Resolve, 3d, If we live to become men, and are intrusted with the office of hiring teachers for youth, or ministers of the gospel, we will patronize none who use, or advocate the use of tobacco.

MR. W.—That will do very well; but we will adjourn now. It is school time.

THE NEW MUFF AND COLLAR.

CHARACTERS:

MR. STUBBS, an honest country farmer.
MRS. STUBBS, a great lover of dress.
MR. URGEM, a city merchant.

SCENE 1.—*A store in Boston.*

MRS. STUBBS.—My dear, you would have forgotten to purchase me a muff, had I not mentioned it to you, and this gentleman says he has some very cheap, and made upon honor.

Mr. Stubbs.—A muff! my dear, you must be too well acquainted with the shortness of my purse, to make such a demand. I have already expended so much by purchasing one nick-nack and another, that I fear we shall be short home.

Mrs. S.—But, dear, what *will* people say if I return without one? It will make a town talk. [*Turning to the merchant.*] You say that you can afford them on reasonable terms?

Mr. U.—Cheaper and better than you can find them in any other place in town. Just look at them. [*Opens a box on the table or counter, and displays some.*]

Mrs. S.—Well, I guess my husband wont object to my taking one, if they are good and cheap, as you say, for he is commonly pretty good natured. [*Turning to her husband.*] Oh, my dear, only see what beauties they are! These are nice. My dear, you *can't* object to my having one, they are so nice.

Mr. S. [*in a low tone*].—I suppose they are very expensive, and why do you urge me to purchase one, when I have not half the money at command?

Mrs. S.—Oh, Mr. Urgem is some acquainted with you, and he seems to be very kind. I dare say he will trust you. [*To the merchant.*] How much *are* your muffs and collars?

Mr. U.—*Only* seventy dollars, ma'am, and they are very fine for that money.

Mr. S.—*Seventy dollars!* the Lord forgive such extravagance as that would be, in us poor folks! My dear, if the muffs are worth that money, let us leave town, for I tell you at once, I can not purchase one without robbing our family of necessaries.

Mrs. S.—Oh, stay one minute. I dare say the gentleman will take off some from the price. Don't be scared at trifles.

Mr. U.—If I do, madam, it will be only that *you* might have one. Wont you take a *muff without* a collar, *that* will come very low? We sell them at only twenty-five dollars. What do you say, sir? [*Turning to Mr. S.*] Come, your lady wishes for one very much, and it will be a great addition to her appearance.

Mr. S.—Why, I say, sir that I am unable to get so

much money by any *honest* means, and as for turning *rogue* to purchase my wife a muff, I shall not do it.

Mrs. S.—Why! now, I think you very unkind. What is the lowest figure you will take?

Mr. U.—Why—really, ah—rather than you should not have one, you may take it at twenty-three dollars.

Mrs. S.—There, now, see how kind he is, and he'll trust you, too. I dare say, he's seen your face in Boston before now—have you not, sir?

Mr. U.—Oh, yes, madam; I have seen him before, I assure you.

Mrs. S.—Come, now, I don't see as you can make one objection, only think now, *only twenty-three dollars*, and you'll make that in some fortunate bargain. Come, my dear, there isn't such a nice muff in Bogtown.

[*Mr. S., silent, turns his back towards Mrs. S., and walks slowly across the floor.*]

Mr. U.—And you *must* have a collar, madam; it will be quite unfashionable not to have one with such a nice muff, and they are very warm and comfortable, I assure you.

Mrs. S. [*to her husband*].—Yes, my dear, I had about as lief have no *muff* as to be without a *collar;* it will look so *unfashionable*.

Mr. U.—Come, sir, I will put them both at sixty-five dollars, and that is absolutely ten dollars less than I can really afford them.

Mrs. S. [*to her husband*].—Come, I see that you *almost* give consent; and will you not take pride now in seeing me look so much nicer than Mrs. Prink, whose furs were called *so* nice?

Mr. U.—Come, do you give your consent that your lady may take one?

Mr. S.—All the consent I shall give, will be not to *quarrel* with my *wife* in *public*.

Mr. U.—Well, sir, as your lady seems to be determined to have one, I think that is about equal to consent.

Mrs. S. [*looking at two or three muffs and collars*].—I think I will take this muff and collar. My husband will settle with you.

Mr. U.—Please give me your name, sir?

Mr. S.—John Stubbs, from Bogtown

SCHOOLDAY DIALOGUES. 37

Mr. U. [*stiffly*].—Ninety days is the longest I give credit.

Mr. S.—Aye, ninety days, I shall not *forget* it, sir, I assure you. [*Exit Mr. and Mrs. Stubbs.*]

Mr. U. [*alone*].—Was not that a fortunate sale to-day. Well, I am lucky for once, and I have realized twenty dollars now. [*Scene closed.*]

Scene 2. *At home.*

Mrs. S.—Come, my dear, will you not go to Mrs. Tibbs with me this evening?

Mr. S.—I thought you didn't care to keep up her acquaintance; strange—though I forgot you have never been there since our trip to Boston.

Mrs. S.—Well, it is so pleasant out, if it is cold; but my furs will keep me so comfortable.

Mr. S.—Well, I never saw such a comfortable article, for I observe that whatever the weather is, the furs appear. They seem to have some good qualities, for I observe you have never been absent from church since you had them; and not only have you been a constant attendant, but you have urged *others* to go. In short, you take vast comfort from them.

Mrs. S.—Of course, I take solid comfort in wearing them, or I would not have got them; but you hard-hearted, close-fisted men are afraid we shall have any thing decent to wear. If you would only take a little interest in ladies' dresses, as some of the people do, how much pleasanter it would be.

Mr. S.—If some ladies would only take a little interest in their husbands' pecuniary affairs, it would be so much better for us. That reminds me that this day I received a bill from Mr. Urgem, saying that a prompt remittance of sixty-five dollars will prevent a presentation of the bill and lawyer's fees, and save much trouble.

Mrs. S.—The unfeeling wretch! Can he doubt your honesty? And am I the cause of so much trouble?

Mr. S.—But, listen. The great trouble with you is, that a whisper in your ear, "There isn't such a nice set of furs in all the town," takes away your better judgment, and just for that sentence I must part with two of my best cows to settle that *small* bill. [*Exit Mrs. S.*]

Mr. S. [*soliloquizes*].—"Misfortunes cluster," and they follow me so closely that were I of that turn of mind, I should give up in despair; but my wife needs a lesson, for she, like many others, just for the sake of having the nicest muff, the costliest gown, the finest bonnet, and the best outside appearance of any in town, would perplex her husband with debts a lifetime. I say this, not that I am austere against the decent fashions, for once I could indulge my wife in most of her wishes. Yes; many I suppose are suffering as I am, and will the ladies ever learn that lesson, not found in schools nor school books, other than that of *experience*, that Christian happiness would feel no mortification at having a finer muff, a finer hat, or a finer dress standing by their own? If their husband's purse require it, they would gain more love and esteem in having their hands muffled up in the skins of their old cats, than in all the furs of the Russian empire. And if experience does not teach them the same lesson, I give them lief to call me old *Pinchpenny* to the end of my existence, which, above all other names, I should dislike, if there is one name I dislike more than another.

CHOOSE YOUR WORDS.

CHARACTERS.

Grandmamma Champney.
Belinda, her granddaughter and namesake.
Lucy, Belinda's twin sister.
Nattie and baby, younger Champneys.
Mrs. Champney.
Nurse White, a h'English woman.

Scene I.—*Nursery. Nurse White, rocking baby to sleep Lucy reading. Nattie building a block-house on the floor. Enter Belinda hurriedly, her dress knocking down Nattie's house. He screams with anger.*

Belinda.—Now, nursey, wont you just sew this ruffle on my dress, and tie on my sash? Mamma has sent for me, and it's the dinner party for grandmamma to-day, you know. Lucy [*throwing her a pair of gloves*], you might mend these; I am so late. It's time I was down stairs, now.

LUCY.—Why didn't you get ready before?

BELINDA.—In the first place, it took me an age to find my things, and then, of course, nothing was ready to put on, and—*do* put down that young one, nurse, and come and help me, or I never shall get dressed.

NURSE [*putting down baby, who sets up a deafening roar*].—Well, Miss B'lindy, though one says it as p'r'aps shouldn't, if you'd h'only be a bit more tidy h'about your h'articles h'of h'apparel, you might ha' been dressed in proper time, and not 'ave set the 'ouse h'in a h'uproar.

BELINDA.—There now, don't stop to talk. Besides, I'm going to turn over a new leaf, for I shall live at the hall most of the time now, since Grandmamma Champney has come there for good. She told mamma that it would renew her own youth to have me there, and mamma cautioned me to be very particular and mind my manners, as grandmamma belongs to the old school, and is very orthodox in her notions.

LUCY.—Do be careful, then, what you say.

BELINDA.—Fudge! Don't you suppose I know beef from a broomstick? Oh dear me! such nice times as I shall have. Only think, Lucy, I shall ride in a coach and four, and the coachman wears a powdered wig, and mamma says her footman is seven feet high! Then she will take me to town, and I shall be presented at court sometime, and all because I happened to be named after her. How lucky it was for me that they did'nt call you Belinda. My apple cart would have been upset, then. Now, Lucy, ain't you sorry?

[*Lucy shakes her head smilingly, and keeps on singing to Nattie's and baby's edification:*]

> What! lost your mitties,
> You naughty kitties,
> Then you shall have no pie.
> Mew, mew, mew, mew, mew!

BELINDA.—How silly! Say, Lucy, now really, ain't you sorry your name isn't Belinda?

Lucy.—I don't know. If it had been, what would you have done? I guess it's all right. You care more for such things than I do.

Nurse [*hooking up Belinda, and nodding her head at Lucy*].—Little saint! 'Ow I wish it were you with h'all my 'eart, so I do. H'its h'always B'lindy, B'lindy, h'all h'over the 'ouse; h'especially h'its so with her mother; but h'Ive a h'idea Miss Lucy'll 'ave the werry 'ighest place h'in 'aeven h'at h'all h'odds.

Belinda.—What a slow coach you are, Nurse! and what's that long string you're mumbling behind my back?

Nurse [*irately*].—Slow coach, h'am h'I! When such, too, as shouldn't be a doin' of it, either, are a slavin' theirselves to death a helpin' of you, and then to be h'insulted h'in this 'ere h'outrageous and h'imperent 'ighfalutinum. I must say, as 'ow h'I—h'I—[*with a great effort*]—I—

Belinda [*laughing*].—All in your eye! Can't you see it in that light?

Lucy.—Now, Belinda, how unkind that is!

Belinda [*with sudden contrition*].—Nursey, you *will* forgive me this time, wont you? You know I didn't mean any thing.

Nurse [*relenting*].—There! I will say, though it's so as perhaps I shouldn't, as 'ow you do 'ave the winningest ways for a fact. But your tongue *may* bring you to sorrow, for h'all that.

Belinda [*shrugging her shoulders*].—Now what's the use of putting it on so thick?

Lucy.—Don't talk so, 'Lindy. Supposing you should say that before Grandmamma Champney.

Belinda.—Say what? Putting it on so thick? You goosey gander, I should be a donkey. What should I want to say that for?

Lucy.—I don't mean just those very words. But you do talk so much *slang*, you know. Now what if you should forget and say such things down-stairs. What *would* be thought of you?

Belinda.—Good little sister Prim, henceforward my words shall travel by special express train, each one labelled "this side up with care." Will that suit?

[*going out*]. Never you fear, but I'll do up business with grandmamma in smashing style.

SCENE 2.—*Drawing-rooms. Ladies and gentlemen standing and sitting in groups, drinking coffee and chatting. Belinda appears in the doorway.*

GENTLEMAN [*stepping up to her*].—Fair, shining spirit whence comest thou? Hast thou strayed from some enchanted realm to bewitch us bewildered mortals here below?

BELINDA [*bridling*].—I am Belinda Champney, sir.

GENTLEMAN [*drawing her forward*].—Ladies and gentlemen, allow me to introduce to your most favorable notice the queen of all the fairies, Miss Belinda Champney. [*All the ladies kiss her.*]

GRANDMAMMA CHAMPNEY [*who sits a little ways back*]. —So that is Belinda. She looked like the Champneys when she was a baby. I see she has all their high-bred beauty. She will be a treasure indeed.

LADY No. 1.—What a little beauty!

LADY No. 2.—What lovely hair!

LADY No. 3.—Such a sweet expression in her eyes!

GENTLEMAN.—Visions of rose-leaves and alabaster drifting in clouds of ærophane will haunt my dreams for evermore. Say, cruel elf, may I get you some coffee, or do they feed you only on dew-drops and nectar?

BELINDA [*quite carried away*].—Not by a long chalk!

GENTLEMAN.—I must believe what you tell me, I suppose.

BELINDA.—We had roast beef to-day and a jolly Yorkshire pudding.

GENTLEMAN.—So, so. True English diet. I shouldn't wonder then, if you played with dolls sometimes, like other earthly maidens.

BELINDA [*disdainfully*].—Indeed, sir, I am much too old to play with dolls. Our governess, Miss McNabon, calls me a young lady.

GENTLEMAN.—And so we study a-b abs, e-b ebs, do we? and are very fond of Miss —Whats-her-name?

BELINDA.—Snap-dragon, I call her, for she's a muff, and crosser than two sticks.

GENTLEMAN.—How hard a lot is yours! You bear your ills most wonderfully well.

BELINDA.—*I* guess I don't study all the time, though Papa gave me a pony last Christmas, and I take a ride every day on him. He can trot 2.40, I'll bet.

GENTLEMAN No. 2.—What a perfect little Di Vernon it is, to be sure! What may this flying steed's name be?

BELINDA.—His name's Garibaldi, and he's a regular trump.

GENTLEMAN No. 2.—Because he appropriates all the tricks, hey?

BELINDA.—He doesn't have any tricks.

GENTLEMAN.—You are too sharp for me. You must be in the habit of taking blades to lunch.

BELINDA.—Nurse always tells us to be careful of the blades.

GENTLEMAN No. 3.—Oh, oh! *now* you are cutting.

GENTLEMAN No. 4.—An original, *en veritas*. Mamma certainly owns no more such prodigies?

BELINDA.—There's Lucy, she's my twin sister, bu she isn't like *me*. Mercy, she's meeker than Moses, and not up to snuff, by any means.

GENTLEMAN No. 4.—Oh! She would only do on a pinch, then.

BELINDA.—Then there's Nattie. But he's one of the small fry, and always in a pickle.

GENTLEMAN.—Let us hope he will be preserved to a green old age.

BELINDA.—And there's the baby. He doesn't do any thing but scream like a house a-fire.

GENTLEMAN No. 4.—He must have a tongue like a roaring flame.

GENTLEMAN No. 1.—Little Nimrod, do you know that I am going to carry you over to my place, bag and baggage, and keep you ever so long.

BELINDA.—I'd like to come, but I'm going somewhere else.

GENTLEMAN.—But I know you'll have a better time at my house. The gold fish talk, and the birds stand still, and wait for you to put salt on their tails.

BELINDA.—Pooh! that's gammon.

GENTLEMAN.—Come, and see if it is. You are never

SCHOOLDAY DIALOGUES.

sure of any thing till you've tried it. Then I have a very nice coachman that will drive you everywhere.

BELINDA. — Grandmamma Champney's coachman drives a four in hand, and I'm going *there*.

GENTLEMAN.—Are there no terms you will listen to?

BELINDA.—No. I know which side my bread is buttered, I guess; and I shall go to grandmamma's.

GENTLEMAN.—You are incorrigible, I see. I shall have to shake hands and leave you. Good-by, then [*Exit ladies and gentlemen.*]

MRS. CHAMPNEY [*hurrying up to Belinda*].—Oh, here you are. I've been looking for you. Your grandmamma wants to take you home with her, now, right away.

BELINDA.—Oh goody!

MRS. CHAMPNEY.—Now, don't be hoydenish; be ladylike and reserved, for she is very precise. Come, she is looking this way [*leads her up to Grandmamma Champney*]. This is Belinda, madam. I trust you will find her to be all you expected.

GRANDMAMMA [*sittiny very straight and speaking stiffly*].—That is settled beyond a doubt.

MRS. CHAMPNEY.—She is said to greatly resemble the Champneys.

GRANDMAMMA [*putting on her spectacles and taking scrutinizing look*].—Yes, yes, I see a Champney nose and mouth, Champney eyes, the true bronze tint in the hair, the proper carriage to the head; all that! But the *mind*—the inward features; think you they could stand the Champney test?

MRS. CHAMPNEY [*nervously*].—Why, yes, I—I think so.

GRANDMAMMA.—Belinda, when you came into the room—and I have watched you from the moment you entered—my heart warmed toward you, for you *looked* a true descendant of our race. The "handsome Champneys" has always been a name well applied to us; but handsome is as handsome does, too, in my eyes; and if the graces of the mind correspond not to those of the body, of what avail is beauty that is only skin deep? [*To Mrs. Champney.*] And now I will trouble you to send for Lucy. I have nothing further to do with Belinda. [*Belinda hides her face in her hands.*]

Mrs. Champney.—But—why—I thought it was Belinda you wanted. She is your namesake. I hope she has not offended you.

Grandmamma.—She is entirely out of the question, after my being an involuntary listener to her conversation a few moments ago. I *might* excuse such language in a stable boy; in a Champney, never.

Mrs. Champney.—Can you not forgive her childish folly for this once? I am sure she will not offend again. [*Lucy enters.*]

Grandmamma.—Lucy, come to me. I can tell by your blushes that you are as modest as the wee woodland flower, whose color deepens in your eyes; and if mamma will spare *you* to me and the old hall, we may soon look to be warmed into life and light by the sunshine of your presence.

Mrs. Champney.—But, madam—

Grandmamma Champney.—Say no more, but allow me to choose Lucy for my protegé and companion, for I feel sure she is worthy of all love and trust. I never should feel safe with one, who knows "which side her bread is buttered," who "snap-dragons" the governess, and goes "2.40" on a "trump" of a pony. I much prefer Lucy, even though she is "meeker than Moses," and indeed this I consider a great recommendation— "that she's not up to snuff," by any means.

THE EFFECTS OF WAR.

CHARACTERS.

Mother.	Henry, a comrade.
Son.	Mother, engaged in sewing
Blanche.	

Scene I.—*Enter son dressed in uniform, the mother looks up in surprise.*

Mother.—My son, what does this mean?

Son.—It means, mother, that your son comes to you this morning, a soldier Our country, my country is in danger! For three long years this bloody war has been upon us, and now there is another call for men. My country calls her sons to her aid; can I refuse? She calls them to rescue her from the grasp of the demon who has her already by the throat; can I hesitate? Can I stand calmly by and hear her cries, and not raise an arm in her defence? No, never!

M.—My son, I fear you do not realize what you do; you are not fit for a soldier; you can not endure the fatigue of the march, and the exposure and privations of the camp; your constitution will soon be broken down, and you will sink into a premature grave.

Son.—Mother, would you withhold your offering from the altar of your country? Think of the Spartan mother who could send away her son to fight for his country, saying, as she gave him his shield, "Return to me with this shield or upon it,"—and would you be less patriotic? No, mother; this strong right arm shall *never* be withheld, when my country calls for me to raise it in her defence. I should despise myself for ever were I to falter because there is personal danger to be encountered.

M.—But think, my son, you are leaving home and friends; friends whose fondest hopes are centered in you, and who have endeavored to make your home a place of sunshine and joy to you; you are leaving them for the battle-field, there perhaps to throw your life away [*wiping a tear*].

S.—No, mother; 'twill not be thrown away; rather given in defence of freedom, and for you and future generations. Seek not to hinder me; my decision is made; my name is on the roll, and I have no desire to withdraw it; much as I love friends and home, with all its hallowed associations, this sacrifice is not *too* great to make for my country.

M.—Well, go, my son, and God be with you, and keep you amid the dangers and temptations of a soldier's life, and hasten the time when you shall return in safety to your home.

S.—Amen! and now good-by. [*They embrace each other, the mother weeping. Exit son. Curtain falls.*]

SCENE 2.—*Charles and Blanche are seated together her hand clasped in his.*

CHARLES.—Dearest Blanche, I must leave you, and I know you will not urge me to stay when my country calls me

BLANCHE.—No, Charles; I will not ask you to stay hard as it is to part. I feel that I would be doing you injustice, as well as disgracing myself. It is our lot to part, and we must submit to it without murmuring.

C.—But ere we part, accept this trifle [*producing a ring and placing it on her finger*], as a token of my love, with the request that it will remind you of the absent one.

B.—And allow me this privilege also [*taking from her own hand a ring and placing it on his*], with the request that you will wear it for my sake.

C.—Your request shall be granted; its sight shall ever call to mind the happy hours spent here; I will part with it but with life, and on the field of battle its sight shall nerve me to greater courage: or, perhaps, when lying on the field of death, its sight shall bring to me thoughts of the loved one at home.

B.—But we will hope to meet again; yet should we not, we will hope to meet above.

C.—And now good-by, I must go [*they embrace each other*]. God bless you!

B.—And you also, and return you safe. [*She accompanies him to the door, where they part, and returning, she covers her face with her handkerchief, and sinks into a chair. Curtain falls*].

SCENE 3.—*A tent, with a musket standing at the door. Charles lies within, dying of a wound received in one of the last battles of the war. Henry, a comrade, bending over him.*

HENRY.—Charles, is there any thing I can do for you?

CHARLES.—Water, give me a drink of water [*he gives him a drink from his canteen*], and now, if you have time, listen to me. You know my condition; take this Bible, and should you live to go home, as I hope you will, give it to my mother, and tell her that I have studied its precepts, and endeavored to obey its commands; tell her that I have done my duty as a soldier, and kept my honor unstained, and I will meet her in a better land. Take this ring, and give it to Blanche; tell her that I have worn it, and as I told her, I part with it but with life: tell her that he who sent it never forgot her, even in his dying hour: tell her, too, not to regret the sacrifice she has made for her country, but rather to feel proud that she gave her lover in defence of her country's cause. But my strength is failing. Good-by. [*Pressing his hand. Curtain falls.*]

SCENE 4.—*Curtain rises. Mother and Blanche are seated together.*

MOTHER.—I wonder why Charles does not write, we have not heard from him for several weeks,

BLANCHE.—As it is nearly time for the mail to arrive, I will go to the office; perhaps we shall get a letter from him [*rising. Enter a soldier*].

SOLDIER [*bowing*].—Mrs. Gray, I believe?

MOTHER.—The same, sir.

S. [*presenting the Bible*].—I bring you——

M. [*springing forward and catching the book*].—My son! my son! you bring me news of him, oh, tell me—tell me all!

S. [*with emotion*].—He bade me give it to you, and tell you that he had done his duty as a soldier, and died as a soldier should.

M.—*Oh my son!* [*pressing the Bible to her heart, and looking up*]. God's will be done.

S.—This, he directed me to give to you [*presenting the ring to Blanche*], and tell you that he never forgot you, even in his dying hour. [*She takes it, and covering her face with her handkerchief leaves the room.*]

PEACE [*advancing*].—Oh war, how dread are thy afflictions! Oh, Columbia, how great the sacrifice which these thy daughters have made for thee! Comfort thee, oh mother; thy son rests among those blessed spirits, who *nobly* cemented our Nation with their blood. Thy sacrifice was great, and thy reward of a nation's gratitude, will also be great. Comfort thee! Thy son perished as a martyr in a glorious cause, and his memory will ever be cherished by a grateful people.

>Sleep on! brave ones who nobly fell
> Upon the gory battle-field;
>Your shroud, naught but a soldier's cloak,
> Your bier, your country's glorious shield:
>
>'eep on! your memory e'er is blest
> By those you nobly died to save;
>\nd many a tributary tear
> Shall fall upon the soldier's grave.

[*Curtain falls.*]

THE TWO INTERPRETERS OF DREAMS.

CHARACTERS.

GRANDMA, arrayed in ancient costume, with spectacles, snuff-box, and knitting.
Girls.—OLIVE, SARAH, MARY, and MAGGIE.
Young ladies.—ALMA and COUSIN EMMA.

Grandma sits quietly knitting, when the girls rush in, asking together:

GRANDMA, grandma, do you believe in dreams?

GRANDMA.—B'leve in dreams, child! why of curse I dew. I b'leve they're most as trew as Scripter. La, me [*snuffing vigorously*]! I've studied my dream-book most every mornin' for sixty yers! B'leve in dreams! I've had so many come round all true, that I'll never doubt them. Why! the night before my poor husband died [*sobbing*], I dreamed that I saw him, so cold and lifeless, and in the mornin' sure enough he was in a ragin' fever. We sent right off for Dr. Slimpton; he lived in the village of Middleburg. [*Stops crying and knits.*] He and Jeremiah used to be great friends; they never had a hard word but once, and that was when Jeremiah thought Simeon Slimpton was paying 'tention to me. Ah! it makes me feel most young to think of those days! [*In her excitement grandma drops a stitch, tries in vain to pick it up, then goes on talking, dropping work.*] What lots of beaux I used to hev! Wal, I wern't bad-lookin'; my cheeks were red as yourn, Olive. My eyes were bright; I could see better then. Here Olive, deary, help your grandmother [*handing her knitting*]. And my hair [*touching the powdered locks*] Ah! Jeremiah used to say these raven locks were enchantin'.

SARAH.—Well! well! Grandma, you were talking awhile ago of sending for Dr. Slimpton. Did grandpa get well?

GRANDMA [*reprovingly*].—Get well! child? how ignorant you are to think he could get well after I dreamed that! No! I knew he couldn't. [*Sobbing.*] And after they sent for the doctor, I went right up stairs to see if my black bombazine would do to wear to the funeral There it had lain in the chest for twenty yers, and was as good as new, and shone like silk. I got Nancy Maria Slimpton to fix it over for me; she charged fifty cents. I think it was shameful on such an occasion. Oh! poor Nancy Maria, she had lots of trouble after I eft there; her nephew's youngest son abused her hamefully and well nigh killed her——

MARY.—Well, grandma, never mind Nancy Maria, now; tell us about our dreams. I dreamed of fire; and oh, how the flames swelled and surged around me! I could not get away, for the doors were all fastened, and the crowd around me was so great.

GRANDMA [*sighing*].—Oh, poor Mary! you will meet with opposition in whatever you undertake, and——

OLIVE.—Oh, grandma! I had an awful dream. I wandered in the woods, and savages were pursuing me, and, in trying to escape, I fell into a den of lions. Oh! they growled and opened their mouths, and then I awoke screaming, and have hardly got over the fright yet!

GRANDMA.—Oh, poor girl! that you have so many enemies, for such means your dream, and all too soon will you be caught in the traps they have set for you. [*Snuffing and sneezing.*] Well, Maggie, child, did you dream?

MAGGIE.—Yes! such an awful dream of my dear soldier brother Robert, that he was at home, and lay so still——

GRANDMA.—Oh! my poor, poor child; so young to bear such a sorrow! Oh, dear! [*Crying and applying handkerchief.*] I dreamed the same when your grandpa died. Oh! how I mourned. May be, now, Maggie, your brother lies in a hospital——

MAGGIE [*wiping her eyes*].—Don't; don't talk so, grandma; you make me feel so bad!

GRANDMA.—Well, well, child, it's all true; dreams are solemn things.

SARAH.—I dreamed last night of Uncle John, that he came home.

GRANDMA [*seeming startled, and rises, dropping her ball and snuff-box*].—Oh! did you?

SARAH.—Yes; and we were so glad to see him.

GRANDMA.—Oh! how strange! for I dreamed the same thing, too. And it's a sure sign we'll never see him again. [*Sobs, and buries her face in her handkerchief.*] Oh, my poor, poor boy! I little thought this hen you bade me good-by, and started for California. Now may be you are dying on a western prairie. Oh! my poor boy! Girls, your old grandmother's heart is broken.

SARAH.—But, grandma, may be he'll come home.

GRANDMA [*sternly*].—Hush! hush, child! Both of us dreamed the same. Dreams never fail. Oh, dear! Oh, dear! [*Departs weeping.*]

SARAH.—There comes Alma. Alma, what makes you look so glad?

ALMA.—Oh! I had a dream.

SARAH.—A dream! a dream! Do you believe in dreams?

ALMA.—Yes; I believe——

OLIVE.—Oh, girls! Alma believes in dreams. Why, Alma, I thought you always laughed about them!

[*All together.*] Oh! goody, goody! I'm glad; now you'll interpret our dreams.

MAGGIE.—We don't like what grandma says, it makes us feel so bad.

MARY.—I dreamed of fire——

ALMA.—Hush! hush girls! you talk so fast. I commenced to say, when you interrupted me, that I believed we dream—[*Girls look disappointed, and exclaim, Oh! is that all? I'm sorry!*]—and that we dream many strange things, and the reason is, we were thinking such thoughts, and they continued even after our eyes closed in slumber. Mary, was it strange you dreamed of fire, when you were reading last night of the great conflagration in the city of Santiago, Chili? The great waste of life there, and the brutality of many, enlisted your sympathies and thoughts.

MARY.—But grandma says I will meet with opposition.

ALMA.—Perhaps you will! but not any more likely because of your dream If Mary meets with opposition.

I hope she will be strong and true, and meet it with a brave heart, remembering that that is what overcomes obstacles.

OLIVE.—I fell into a den of lions; and grandma said that meant I had many enemies.

ALMA.—Of course you would dream of lions, after reading Dr. Livingstone's travels in Africa, and his adventures with the king of beasts. And as for enemies, if you are loving, kind and true, and do to others as you would have them do to you, enemies will not harm you.

MAGGIE.—Oh, Alma! do you believe that my brother is in the hospital? I dreamed he was sick.

ALMA.—No, no, child! You were writing to him before retiring, and thinking perhaps danger would befall him.

SARAH.—Grandma and I both dreamed of Uncle John, and she went off just now in a fit of hysterics, because she says it is a sure sign he is dead.

ALMA.—Nonsense! Grandma is whimsical. She has thought and fancied so much about dreams, and that there was reality in them, that she makes both herself and others miserable. I hope you never will be so carried away by them, and borrow trouble about the future. Dreams are very pleasant, if we view them in a sensible light. I heard cousin Emma read something about them yesterday.

GIRLS.—Oh, I would like to hear it! Wont she read it to us?

ALMA.—I'll go after her. [*Goes and returns soon with cousin Emma.*]

EMMA.—Well, girls, you see Alma has really "pressed me into the service," so I'll not retreat, but do the best I can. [*Reads.*]

DREAMS.

"Come, Winnie, and sail on the River of Sleep,
 Where the fair Dream Islands be."

Sleep may be likened to a broad, calm, beautiful river on which we sail at eventide, when twilight's dim, leaden mantle has changed to a darker hue. In our light barks we float calmly along, without a ripple or wave to disturb us, when the toils of the day are over. This river is studded with fair and beautiful Dream Islands. Oh the beauty with which they are adorned! We view their grand and delightful scenes, flashing rivers, crystal lakes, flowers with rare and sweet perfume, and birds with gay plumage and sweetest songs.

And while our bark stops there, and we revel in the beauty and grandeur, we forget all worldly cares and annoyances. All with pure and holy thoughts may enjoy the beauty without money and without price. And very thankful am I for that. For the poor forget their pinching poverty. The longing eyes, which so delight in nature's grand and beautiful scenes, but are debarred from them, may now feast heart and soul. Those who are separated from friends may again meet and commune with them. But even to some who sail on the river are beauties denied. To those whose lives are spent in selfish idleness, base crime, or those who daily drink of the maddening bowl—to these, dire serpents sluggishly move the waters, and ferocious beasts start from the green thickets with glaring eyes and opened mouth. And madly trying to dispel the scene, the almost delirious victims of sin curse the River of Sleep, and even the fair Dream Islands. But to the good they prove a blessing. Ever flow thou on, peaceful river, set with emerald gems!

SARAH.—Alma, you said you had a dream. Tell it to us, and what makes you seem so happy.

ALMA.—Well, Sarah, I will answer you by repeating a poem which I love dearly, and then we must go to our lessons. [*She repeats:*]

"Pleasant were my dreams last night,
Till the dawn of morning light;
All the lonely midnight hours
Roamed I Dream-land's fairy bowers.

And the friends of Long Ago,
Those I loved and cherished so,
Looked on me with loving eyes,
Clasped my hand in glad surprise.

Tender words, like holy balm,
Filled my soul with heavenly calm;
Sweeter than the song of birds,
Seemed to me those loving words.

"But the joy within my heart,
Does not with the night depart,
Tender words my spirit thrill,
Loving eyes look on me still.

"I've been humming all day long
Snatches of an old time song;
Know you why my heart is light;
Pleasant were my dreams last night.

"*Surely blessed are those hours,
When, like dew upon the flowers,
Full they on the weary, sleeping;
Saddest eyes forget their weeping.*"

THE FOUR SEASONS.*

[The curtain rises, and a little girl appears dressed in white with scarf and sash of pink, a crown of small flowers on her head, and bouquets in her hand. She speaks:—]

I am Spring. They call me beautiful Spring. My step is light and my voice is glad. I love all that is young; I cheer all that is old. I call sweet flowers to light among the gray old rocks, and make the green leaves to tremble in their loveliness, among ancient ruins.

I bring not only soft, light, fresh winds, green leaves, and fair flowers with me, but young birds in their nests, and young lambs to play in the meadows.

Little fishes dart about in the brooks, too, and frogs sing in the marshes. I come like Hope to the people They hear my voice, and lay the seed in the ground, and trust it to the dew and the sunshine, the rain and the smile of God.

I am a miracle worker on earth, and a type of the fadeless land toward which mortals journey.

The prisoner in a gloomy dungeon far away, feels my breath on his brow, and thinks of the rolling floods, and the glad joy in that mountain home in whose defence his comrades fell, for whose sake he can smile at imprisonment and death. In my smile he hopes.

Now he says, "It is Spring time, and my brothers and friends will gird on their armor and come and liberate me."

The Father above, who guides the young birds back to their last year's haunts, careth too for me, and it is Spring. Lights and shadows fell on the way of the red breast as he journeyed northward, but he hoped and trusted; he was true as Spring, and Spring is as true as God.

I am crowned with flowers; I am laden with them; I am joyous and fair; I am a being of light, and melody, and fragrance.

I am the beautifier of Nature, the beloved of man, a visible promise of Paradise. In Heaven only may I tarry.

---

* This Dialogue was written in 1863.

Here I come, but to depart. I must away, away to make room for my lovely sister, the Summer; but forget me not. I am Spring, beautiful Spring.

[Scattering the flowers, she departs.]

[Enter Summer—A large girl in a pink dress and scarf, and sash of green, and a broad-brimmed straw hat wreathed with roses. On her left arm a small sheaf of wheat, in her right hand a sickle. She says:—]

I am Summer, gay, and bright, and gleesome. "Laughing Summer" I am called. I have the brightest sunshine, the thickest canopy of leaves, the stillest, warmest air about me, and the bluest sky above.

I come to the lands of the North like a dream of tropical beauty. I call the dwellers of the city out into the forest haunts. I fill their souls with my glory. Young maidens are ever garlanded with flowers in my reign; and I hear the children's laughter ringing out on the air that is so sweet, wandering over orchards bright with clover blossoms, and meadows sweet with new mown hay.

Happy Summer I am called. I fill the children's hands with strawberries. I load the trees with cherries for shouting boys to shake down into the aprons of bright-eyed little girls.

In my smile the apples grow rosy and mellow, and the farmer's face is glad as he gathers the golden pears. It is when my step is abroad in the land that the poet weaves his brightest vision, and the patriot's devotion is truest.

It is then he looks abroad and says: "My native land! my own, my native land!" and "Where's the coward that would not strike for such a land?" I am the friend of the patriot soldier. The youth, on the lonely rounds of his picket duty, blesses God for me. Looking up to my starry sky, he thinks how, in his far-off home, the eyes of dear ones rest on those same bright sentinels of heaven, the while they pray for him.

Yes, I am Summer, the radiant and happy, even though there is war in the land; for Peace will come over the land at last like Summer and the Sun of Peace shall shine as my sun at noonday. The eagle shall spread his wing on the mountain unfearing; the earth shall be glad and rejoice; the reapers shall be many, and the harvest plenteous. This is the voice of the passing Summer.

[AUTUMN—A young girl in dress of buff or corn color, with blue sash and scarf, and crowned with wheat or Autumn leaves and grasses; in her hand a horn of plenty.]

I am Autumn. Spring promised, and Summer brought, but I finish.

They call me mellow Autumn, and jolly Autumn, and I, too, am loved. When barns and cellars are full, all hearts are happy. The blossoms of Spring were fair, and the roses of Summer bright; but my wild flowers are of gold and purple, and scarlet, royal, and radiant.

I have strewn the wood paths with dry leaves, I have warned the dear birds that it was time to be gone southward; but the chatter of squirrels over their hoarded treasures is heard in the woods, and the voices that go up from the streams are pleasant, the grasshopper's song is ended, and the bee hums near its hive.

The girls have gathered the grapes, and the boys the nuts; the plough is tracing the furrows over the brown fields, and the farmer's table is graced by bread from his land, and honey from his hives.

And my winds are wild and stirring in their tones:

"They have been across red fields of war,
  Where shivered helmets lie,
They have brought me thence the thrilling note,
  Of a clarion in the sky;
A rustling of proud banner-folds,
  A peal of stormy drums—
All these are in their music met
  As when a leader comes."

Oh! what is like rich, ripe, mellow Autumn, in a land that God has blessed among the nations—a land whose starry banner shall float over it, when its people shall indeed be free?

This, oh land of beauty, is the prophecy of Autumn!

SCHOOLDAY DIALOGUES.

[WINTER—A boy representing an old man arrayed in an ample black cloak, trimmed with white fur—with gray hair streaming from beneath a heavy fur cap—a pair of skates swung from his shoulder.]

I am Winter. I brought the snow, and the boys shouted hurrah; the girls clapped their hands rosy with the cold, and said: "Ha! ha!" I traced the pictures of wondrous beauty on the window panes, and bridged rivers, and hung pearls on the pine trees.

I set my winds to shouting, and quickened everybody's steps. My snow flakes whirl, my snow birds flutter by, and my clouds hurry.

It is I that have the Christmas tree to decorate my halls, and the New Year's fire to blaze on my hearth, and then the little cricket chirrups there, while the turkey roasts, and the apples and nuts are heaped in the basket.

Oh! the boys get their skates now, and hurrah for the sport! And the girls may come along too, and listen to the sleigh bells! what fun! hurrah! To be upset in the snow-drifts, ah, that is merry!

Yes, I am Winter, and most welcome to all, no thanks to fair young Spring, bright Summer, and mild Autumn to be cheerful; but for Winter, an old man to come with such grace and pleasantry, that all are glad to see him—that is fine! O Winter, Winter, happy is the country that rejoices in thee!

The merriest games are played in my long evenings, the sweetest songs are sung then, and the best stories told.

Beautiful are the shadows that the fire-light casts on the wall, and "pleasant and mournful to the soul the memory of joys that are past!"

I bade you rejoice, but I bid you also to mourn—to mourn for those whose deaths have made hearths safe and holy—those peasant men who became warriors at their country's call.

Let the records of their bravery be eternal! While ever your homes are dear, praise ye the men who perished to preserve them, and let Winter beseech you to care for the widow and orphan.

Under the cold light of my stars, their homes seem doubly desolate, and my winds to them take the sound of bitter wailing.

I am Winter, and 'tis my voice that asks you to care for the poor, who have offered up their beloved on the altar of sacrifice, and while you pray "O God be merciful!" be ye merciful, give, give—it is laying up treasures in heaven.

Winter is the friend of Freedom. Amid the snowy Alps, the undaunted Tell, with his friends, defied the tyrant; and at Valley Forge the patriotism and the heroism of Washington and his army were sublime and God-like. Shall the descendants of such fathers hold Liberty less dear?

[Spring, Summer, and Autumn appear again, and clasping hands with winter, form a circle. Winter proceeds:—

"It is your banner in the skies,
  Through each dark cloud that breaks,
And mantles with triumphant dyes,
  Your thousand hills and lakes.

This is the voice of the whole year.

[*The curtain falls.*]

SCHOOL AFFAIRS IN RIVERHEAD DISTRICT.

CHARACTERS.

SQUIRE WISEMAN,
JOB TURNER, and } School Committee.
HANS SCHWEITZER,
JOSEPH HARRIS, an accomplished gentleman **and Teacher.**
SAM PRICE the preference of the Board.
PUPILS.

SCENE 1.—*Harris and his Scholars.*

HAR.—My dear pupils! I desire to say a few words to you, before I dismiss the school to-night. You have all done well to-day, and I love to encourage you. Do you not all feel better after doing a good day's work?

SCHOOLDAY DIALOGUES.   59

Pupils.—Yes, indeed.

Har.—I know you do. I knew just what you were going to say. Work does us a great deal of good. It makes the blood course freely in our veins. It makes our cheeks glow. It is better than medicine, because it prevents many ills. It does us good to *think* about good deeds And I know you all feel better, to-night because you have a good day's work to think about. Don't you all love to study and learn hard lessons? If any boy or girl, in my school, does not like to spend his time well, does not feel better when he has worked hard, and has done something, let him raise his hand. [*One hand is raised.*]

Har.—Well, Charlie, speak out. Do you not feel better when at work?

Charlie.—Not a bit of that. I feel best when I am *wabblin* about.

Har.—Come here, Charlie. I like to see you honest I love honest boys. Always speak the truth. I like to see you all active. Charlie doesn't understand me. He thinks I am commending boys who are always still. I do not mean that. Industry requires activity. Industrious students, however, are industrious thinkers. And thought is silent. [*Another hand is raised.*] What do you want to say, James?

James.—Do thoughts always keep still?

Har.—Not always. They often seek expression. But much talking indicates little thought. We ought to express our thoughts; but look out for proper occasions. You may recollect the proverb which says: "Still waters run deep." To turn upon another subject: I am sorry to think, scholars, that we are so perplexed about classing and teaching you properly. Our books have become so various, that I find it very difficult to teach as I would like. I do not find as much time for each class, as I could if our system of books, studies, etc., were improved. But let us be patient. I intend to see Squire Wiseman, the most prominent and influential man of the school board, and see what can be done to better our condition. In the meantime, let us work hard to get our lessons well. We will close school by repeating a few of James Montgomery's questions and answers [*School divides—one class on the right and one on the left of the stage.*]

1st *class.* Nature, whence sprang thy glorious frame?
2d *class.* My Maker called me and I came.
1st *class.* Oh, Sun! what makes thy beams so bright!
2d *class.* The word that said, "Let there be light."
1st *class.* Planets, what guides you in your course?
2d *class.* Unseen, unfelt, unfailing force.
1st *class.* Flowers, wherefore do you bloom?
2d *class.* We strew thy pathway to the tomb.
1st *class.* Dews of the morning, wherefore are ye given?
2d *class.* To shine on earth, then rise to heaven.
1st *class.* Time, whither dost thou flee?
2d *class.* I travel to eternity.
1st *class.* Oh, Life! what is thy breath?
2d *class.* A vapor lost in death.
1st *class.* Oh, death! how ends thy strife?
2d *class.* In everlasting life.

Har.—School is dismissed. [*All pass out.*]

Scene 2.—*Mr. Harris, Squire Wiseman and Job Turner*

Har.—How are you, my good friend? I have been desirous of meeting *you* for some time. I have much which concerns the common interests of our school and district to converse about. I fear we shall not have time for all.

Sq. W.—Perhaps not. But it doesn't matter. I am not very well versed in these school affairs, you know. And a conversation would not be of much service to you, it may be. However, I shall be happy to meet you, at the office, some evening.

Har.—That will not do. I have little time for any thing merely promotive of my *own* pleasure. I must improve a moment, at present, I think, hoping that you will pardon the impropriety there may be in urging it. I have been thinking of trying to remove a difficulty under which we labor respecting books.

Sq. W.—What difficulties do the books make! I thought they were made to *remove* difficulties.

Har.—So they were. Yet some do their work but poorly enough—making more than they *remove.*

Sq. W.—How is that? How is that? Are you get

ding so wise as to know more about books than the book-makers?

HAR.—I can tell, I think, when a book serves a good purpose as a text, and when not.

SQ. W.—Well! well! How are you going to mend things? The law will not allow you to interfere with our books.

HAR.—'Tis true; and most properly is such interference, on my part, prohibited. But I wish to influence you, and those associated with you, as a school committee, to the fulfillment of *your* duty respecting this matter. I would like to see the very wise provisions of our law enforced, respecting a *uniformity* at least.

SQ. W.— I never could see much force in the statute to which you refer.

HAR.—Indeed! Perhaps you have not reflected upon its importance. To me it is one of the most essential and important features of the code.

SQ. W.—I generally look at the importance of things, sir. I should not be qualified to act as umpire for others, were it not the case.

HAR.—Let me then call your attention to the great want of classification, existing in our school, when I first took charge of it—a want, too, which still exists, and which is occasioned, solely, on account of the variety of text-books used by pupils of the same age and advancement.

SQ. W.—Well, I can't see how it matters about the book, if pupils be well and correctly taught.

HAR.—True! but how can they be well taught in such a case as mine?

SQ. W.—Hem! Well, if people have books, they will hardly trouble themselves to get more.

HAR.—But they should. And, by the law, they are bound to, if prescribed by the right authority. The *convenience* of *one* should be sacrificed to the *necessities* of the *many*.

SQ. W.—Oh, well! I fear you can't introduce these new-fangled notions among *us*. We are a steady, straight-forward people. Don't go in for change.

HAR.—Except *pocket* change! *I* do not desire to introduce such notions as those, of which you speak

The law has anticipated *me* in the premises, looking, as it did, to the pressing demands of the youth of our schools. *I* would like to see its wise provisions *executed*. I, therefore, appeal to you as the authorized agents of the law-making power to attend to our wants. I should be glad to give any advice that would assist you in the adjustment of our difficulties.

[*Enter Job Turner, another member of the school ommittee.*]

Tur.—What advice is that ar you propose to give to us? I heard you had gone over to stir up a fuss, and I thought I'd come over and see tew it. We don't want men around here who can't attend to their own business.

Har.—I am surprised, Mr. Turner. All that I have done, I have done with honest intentions. I am not aware that I have overstepped the bounds of my duty.

Tur.—Is it your business to run down our schoolhouse?

Har.—It is my duty to call attention to what I believe to be for the good of the school.

Sq. W.—Why, Mr. Harris, what *is* the matter with our house? We *all* got our education in it.

Har.—It may be. But it is now grossly dilapidated.

Tur.—Now I am a new hand in this business. But I know such things as these will make trouble.

Har.—I must go. I hope we shall all do our best in our respective capacities to meet all the warts of those under our care. [*Exit Harris.*]

Sq. W.—Now, Job, this is insulting. We can't stand this. I am not penurious—but—but let us quietly get rid of this man. I can, perhaps, induce him to resign

Tur.—Go it, squire. I am in. I'll be bound if we wont show him that *he* can't rule all Riverhead. After we git him out, we'll have an examination and employ accordin' to our own notions.

Scene 3.—*Squire Wiseman, J. Turner, H. Shweitzer, and Samuel Price. Examination day.*

Sq. W.—I suppose you heard of the resignation of Mr. Harris as teacher in our school.

SCHOOLDAY DIALOGUES.

Tub.—I did that. It takes you, squire, for them things. I heard to-day there was an examination, and I thought I'd come up in time to get posted.

Sq. W.—Well, I don't like to talk about myself. But somehow or other, I always thought I could manage all these delicate affairs with some success. Eh?

Tub.—Exactly, squire. And I must say I felt kinder proud to be elected school committee with you. You see, I knew that affairs would go on *swimmingly*, as long as *you* manage them. [*Squire struts about with importance.*]

Sq. W.—Yes—Yes. Wall, I hope they will.

Tub.—Oh! I know they will. Don't talk to me, when the squire is in for any thing. It's all right. I need to learn.

Sq. W.—All right, neighbor. We ought to move carefully in these matters.

Tub.—Yes, I reckon we had. Look what everlastin' musses are kicked up sometimes, because things aint arranged as they orto be.

Sq. W.—So, so. The time for the examination has nearly arrived. Let me tell you one thing, Job. Let us all work together. Our friend, Schweitzer, who is one of the committee, as you are aware, is very strong in his opinions, sometimes. And, under such circumstances, it will be better to sacrifice our own notions, you know, in order to preserve harmony.

Tub.—Well, I reckon so, too. But there are some pints about teachin' that I allow to know a heap about, and I'd like to have my say, you know.

Sq. W.—Oh, certainly! We all have that privilege. [*Enter Schweitzer.*]

Schw.—Goot afternoon. Vot for ye talkin' so much Ish it not time for de examination?

Tub.—Don't get into a flurry now. We're goin' to sarve the public now. We must look——

Schw.—Vot for you look so long? You never do de vork in dis vay. I must go home in one hour to sow my turnips. So hurry on.

Sq. W.—As soon as our friends, the teachers, come, we will proceed.

Schw.—Vell, den. Here comes a poor tivil of a

schoolmaster, I know. Ax him a few quibbles, and if he can't answer noting, praps he can teach the young uns to spell. [*Enter Sam Price, applicant for a school.*]

Sq. W.—Take a seat, sir. [*Teacher gawks about, and finally sits down with his hat on.*]

Tur.—Well, squire, do you know this man? I reckon he *is* arter a school.

Sq. W.—I suppose so. Friend, did you see our notice?

Price.—Yās, I did. I thought I'd come up.

Schw.—Vot for you come up? Can you teach school?

Tur.—Hold on, now. We are goin' into a regular examination in a minnit. All these things 'll come out then. I am goin' in for first-rate disqualifications.

Schw.—Vell, den, go to vork. I no go in for so much zamination, or vot you call him.

Tur.—Come, Squire, this is your business. [*Squire looks wise and proceeds.*]

Sq. W.—What is your name?

Price.—Samuel Price, sir.

Schw —Who cares for de name? 'Tis de teacher we want.

Sq. W.—What is the place of your nativity?

Price.—What is it, sir?

Tur.—Where did you live when you was born? he says.

Price.—I don't remember. I guess 'twan't far off.

Sq. W.—Where were you educated?

Price.—I don't jest understand you.

Schw.—Vare did you larn noting? he says.

Price.—I larnt some at school—but *more* sence I got out on't.

Tur.—Have you got any more *sense* than you used to have?

Price.—I saved a little change in teachin' down country.

Sq. W.—Then you have had some experience?

Price.—Oh, yas!

Sq. W.—Did you please the people?

Price.—I don't know. Spect I did.

SQ. W.—Will you read some for us? Here is a book. *Reads awkwardly but very loud. Job Turner gets perfectly astonished at the fine elocution.*]

TUR.—Good gracious, mister! Where did you larn to read like that? It beats every thing I ever dreamed of. I reckon you *can* teach some, can't ye? You see we all go in for the very best kind o' larnin' about here—cipherin', spellin', and the like. That sounds more like real edication than any thing I've listened to in a long time. Excuse me, squire; really I didn't mean to disturb you.

SQ. W.—What's grammar?

PRICE.—Grammar is the way things is done—perticulerly in the matter of speakin', talkin', riten', etc.

SQ. W.—How is it divided?

PRICE.—Among the scholars accordin' to their ages

SQ. W.—What is a noun?

PRICE.—Any thing you can hear, feel or taste.

SCHW.—Yes, and *schmell*, too, I b'leve.

SQ. W—What is a verb?

PRICE.—A verb is what bees, doos, suffers, ax, and passes.

SQ. W.—What verbs are transitive?

PRICE.—Some verbs is transitive, and some isn't.

SQ. W.—Will you do some geometry for us?—any thing you please.

PRICE.—Oh, yās. The four sides of an icicle triangle is about equal to three right angles; and a round circle aint got no end.

SQ. W.—Well, that will do, unless the other gentlemen have questions to ask.

SCHW.—Oh, no, it ish goot—betters as I have heard in a long time.

TUR.—We have heard enough to satisfy us, I reckon

SQ. W.—Will you please to retire! [*Price passes out.*]

SQ. W.—Well, what do you think? I don't exactly like the appearance of the man.

SCHW.—He looks well enough. 'Tis te teacher we want.

SQ. W.—But the address of a man has a great influence upon pupils.

Tur.—*He's smart, though;* aint he, squire?

Sq. W.—Yes, rather apt, though his answers were not all correct. Still—we—have been paying rather too high. If this man will teach for a reasonable salary I am willing to employ him—say *ten dollars a month.*

Schw.—I go for ten dollars a mont, too. 'Tis pig brice I know. But the poor tivil must live.

Tur.—I am willin' to agree to what's fair in his case. Ten dollars is above my mark, some two dollars. But I see he is a goin' to do up the business right, and I am willin' to agree to the price.

Sq. W.—Inform him, Mr Turner, of his appointment and if he accepts, he can commence immediately.

Schw.—Squire, you see dat dis deacher puts in de whole time. We no wants to lose money on dis pargain, nohow. [*Exit all.*]

Scene 4.—*Sam Price in school. Pupils talking loud and noisy.*

Price.—Silence!!! D'ye hear that? Set down!! Take off your hats!! Ef ye don't be still now, I'll use that hickory to your hearts' content, ye young —— Class in jogerphy, come up. [*Pupils come shuffling and crowding.*] Where do you live?

Class.—At home.

Tea.—Right; but in what town? I meant.

Cl.—Don't know.

Tea.—Riverhead.

Cl.—Riverhead. Riverhead. Riverhead.

Tea.—What's the shape of the earth?

Cl.—Of a punkin shape.

Tea.—What motion has it?

Cl.—It goes on an axle-tree, and has a motion bigger yet.

Tea.—What town in the Great Desert?

Cl.—Egypt.

Tea.—What State in New York?

Cl.—Varmount.

Tea.—Class dismissed.

Pupils.—May I go *out*? Please, *may I* go *out*? Master, let *me* go *out*? Tom's pinchin'. Master, may I tell you on Jim? He's ben doin' somethin', etc.

Tea.—Yes, yes. *All go out.* [*All run—two or three fall down. Teacher rings a bell repeatedly, but no scholars come in. Soliloquizes.*] Plague on the varmints. I'll lick 'em. I wonder if I *wăs* born to teach school, any how? That's what they all say. But I don't believe it, jest. Here I am, and nobody to listen to my valuable instructions. I'll go and resign———. No I wont either. Dad and mam 'll laugh too much to see me comin' hum now. I give fust, best kind o' satisfaction among the people. They all say I beat the other teacher—Harris—all to nothin'. They had to turn him out. He kicked up the greatest fuss about this old house, books, and other foolish things, ever I heerd tell on. I'm thinking ef he warnt about right, tew. We have got the scurviest old house in creation, I reckon. But a feller can get on in these ere parts, ef he only has the larnin'. That's what puts me through. I know how it goes by experience. But if I could only make these varmints toe the scratch, I'd go it slick as ile. Only keep dark about matters furrin to real teachin', and a feller can become popular in these diggins—just as easy —That's so [*Rings.*] Confound the *ung uns.* I wish the old Harry had 'em, and I was in *Hardscrabble* agin 'long with the old folks. Wouldn't I get drunk on apples and cider, and go to see Sally, eh? Wouldn't I be up to that? Oh, yes! Thar's them boys goin' into that orchard. [*Takes his hat and runs back and forth.*] I'll haze 'em. [*Runs back for his whip.*] I'll lick 'em Dogs and all mustard! I'll bring 'em up and see if they'll go away agin. Ef I don't lam 'em! [*Leaves.*]

NOVEL READING.

CHARACTERS.
Lena Grey. Her brother.
Frank Grey.
Edgar Ramon.

Edgar.—Will you please tell me what book you are reading, Lena? I have been regarding your countenance for sometime, and by its ever varying expression I judge you are much interested.

LENA.—I am interested; it is the most fascinating story I ever read.

EDGAR.—Will you please tell me the character of the book? I can not consider it one that requires much profound study; you turn the leaves too rapidly.

FRANK.—Her glances are quick and comprehensive; a very few convey to her mind all the information she desires.

LENA.—The book is a novel, I suppose; for it contains the usual amount of love, jealousy, sentiment, and crime; but do you think it is wrong to spend a little time occasionally in reading merely for amusement?

EDGAR.—That depends upon the kind of amusement the book affords. We would not pelt ourselves with stones for the sake of obtaining exercise; nor should we permit the mind to indulge in recreation equally injurious.

LENA.—Most surely you would not imply that because I indulge in novel reading, I shall render myself less capable of performing the trivial duties of daily life. With the greatest economy of time I can obtain only a few hours each day for mental culture; and should I spend even the greater part of that in novel reading, what evil could result from it?

EDGAR.—In the words of the learned Daniel Wise, let me reply, "Obscured, feeble intellect, a weakened memory, an extravagant and fanciful imagination, benumbed sensibilities, a demoralized conscience, and a corrupted heart."

LENA.—Could I believe that all that troop of evils would follow so harmless a pastime, I would never again unfold the covers of a novel.

FRANK.—Were success even possible, I would try to convince you of the truth; but you are so persistent in the maintenance of an agreeable tenet, that I fear you would employ your inclination rather than reason in forming a conclusion.

LENA.—If I have ever given you occasion to form such an opinion of me, I certainly regret it; but why should novel reading obscure the intellect? We are brought in contact with some of the most lovely and pure beings that the imagination can conceive; we trace their conduct through an ever eventful life; we observe the motives that controlled their acts; and are we not benefited? We are also led to contemplate viler shades of character. We behold ignorance, misery, vice, and crime; we trace their origin; they excite our loathing; and we discern more clearly the excellence of virtue.

FRANK.—I should certainly rejoice could I believe that you had been so benefited.

EDGAR.—Novels address themselves to the passions and there is great danger that we shall sympathize not only with the pure and lovely characters portrayed by the novelist, but also with those that are less worthy. Thieves, profligates, and murderers, are represented as shrewd, ingenious, and talented; and the fact that they possess qualities that are admirable, renders them objects of greater interest to us. We regard such characters as necessary to form an agreeable contrast with the more angelic beings; and the more deeply they are cast in blood and crime, the more pleasing is the effect.

LENA.—How can the study of such contrasts disaffect the mind? May we not admire the talent that enables a man to accomplish a bad purpose, and yet despise the doer?

EDGAR.—Novels are not read merely for the purpos of observing the contrasts of character presented there nor for criticism; but, as you have said, "for amusement." They fill the mind with lively pictures of what might be true; and yet the utter improbability that a person would ever be placed in similar circumstances renders it useless that we should burden our memory with a record of the lives portrayed there.

LENA —There is one excellency, at least, that I trust you will accord to novels; they certainly tend to make the imagination more vivid.

FRANK.—My dear sister, I deeply regret your apparent ignorance in regard to the adaptation of words Assuredly, you would not have used the adjective "lofty," instead of "distorted," had you considered how illy it expressed your meaning.

EDGAR.—There are many most excellent works of the imagination; the productions of the most gifted minds; Such might well repay our perusal. But novel reading intoxicates our minds rather than elevates our conceptions; for, even as the inebriate, jovial with wine, fancies he has attained the height of happiness, so the novel reader, lost in the mazes of fiction, believes that all the longings of her mind are satisfied. Then, too, reading should be pursued for benefit, and ladies are seldom deficient in imagination.

FRANK.—That is certainly true. If all Lena's plans could have been carried into effect, our earth would have been an Eden, our home a paradise, long ago.

LENA.—Do you condemn all works of fiction?

EDGAR.—No; there are some fictitious writings most excellent in their character. I would object only to those which leave the mind in an excited, unsatisfied state, which "rob us of a higher pleasure than they afford, since the same attention to solid reading would procure us loftier, purer pleasures."

LENA.—Your argument is specious; but I certainly do not like to believe it. I will not decide immediately on so important a question.

FRANK.—You will rather wander awhile in the ditch in order to see if you will be defiled.

LENA.—No; I will stand on the bank and consider.

THE DEMONS OF THE GLASS.

CHARACTERS.

JAMES PENNINGTON and } drinking friends.
JERRY SPENCER,
TOTIE, a fairy.
POVERTY.
CRIME.
DISEASE.
EDITH.
LITTLE CHILD and SERVANT.

SCENE 1.—*Enter Pennington and Spencer.*

PENNINGTON.—Now, Jerry, sit down and have something before you go down street. This is a raw day out, you know.

SPENCER.—I can stay but a few minutes, Pennington

You are aware that I must meet my father at the depot in—let me see—[*takes out his watch*]—just fifteen min utes. [*They both sit down at a table.*]

PENN.—This would be a cold world, indeed, Jerry, if we couldn't have a little something warm to take occasionally, you know. [*Rings the bell.*] Good whisky, Jerry, is the best thing in the world to develop the latent caloric in the human system, physiologically speaking. [*Enter servant.*]

SERVANT.—Did you ring, sir?

PENN.—Yes, I rang. Bring us some of that best whisky, Tom. Mind, the best. Of course I rang. Didn't you know what to bring, without coming to see?

SERVANT.—I might have known. [*Aside.*] He doesn't want much else but whisky any more.

PENN.—Quit your muttering there, and bring the whisky.

SERVANT.—Yes, sir. [*Exit.*]

SPENCER.—It's well to have a good friend, Pennington, and I've often thought that we ought to look to each other's interests a little more. James Pennington, I believe we are both indulging in the glass too much. For my part, I have determined to quit short off. When I drink this time with you—[*enter servant with two glasses, filled, on a waiter, and exit*]—it shall be the last.

PENN.—What! why, Jerry, whisky's a great institution. It's the life and soul of a man almost. [*Takes up glass and hands it to Spencer; takes the other himself; both rise.*] Here's health, Jerry, and may you never think less of me for saying, Here's to your resolution!

SPENCER.—May you never live to realize the tortures of the "Demons of the Glass!" [*Pennington drinks. Spencer, unnoticed, cautiously throws the contents of his glass upon the floor.*] So now, Pennington, good-by. I must go.

PENN.—Good-night, Jerry. Stop and see me often. [*Exit Spencer.*] "Demons of the Glass!" What does he mean? I feel very strange to-night. I don't think I'm drunk. I've been drunk before, and I didn't feel this way. Pshaw! doctors often recommend whisky—

say it's good for consumption. Well, so it is, good for
my consumption, for I do consume it sometimes, that's
certain. Ha! Ha! that's a g-o-a-k [*spelled only*] as
friend A. Ward has it. [*Rings bell*]. Whisky is good.
" I like it," as an old hotel-keeper out West used to say.
Good to raise the spirits. [*Three or four distinct raps
near the table. Starts in his chair, astonished.*] Hallo!
what's that! Spirits raised sure enough. [*Enter servant with glass on waiter.*] You're a good fellow, Tom.
When I shuffle off this mortal coil—die, I mean—I'll
leave you all my old clothes. [*Drinks.*]

SERVANT [*aside*].—He won't have much else *to* leave
any body, if he keeps going on at this rate.

PENN.—You're a good fellow, Tom; bring me another
glass of this soul-reviving elixir of life.

SERVANT [*aside*].—*He likes " er"* that's true! [*Aloud.*]
Another, sir?

PENN.—I—said—hic—another—didn't I? An—hic—
'nother! Of course another. [*Exit servant.*] Another
—hem! why not? Whisky is a fundamental princ-
—hic—ciple. What's a fellow to do if there's no spirit
in him. Another? I can afford—hic—to drink as much
as I please. I'm a—hic—able. I'm rich. I'm going to
marry the handsomest, the richest, the most intelligent
lady in the city. I'm going to—to—be the happiest
man alive—[*enter servant with glass—Pennington takes
it*]—if Edith Graham and this can make me. You
didn't put just a little too much water in this, did you,
Tom?

SERVANT.—No, I *hope* not. [*Exit.*]

PENN. [*sets the glass on the table and looks at it*].—
Jerry said something about " Demons of the Glass." I
don't see any. Jerry's a good fellow, and when he said
that, he must have meant something. I feel very strange
sleepy, and drowsy. [*Thoughtfully and low.*] "Demons
in the glass." [*Falls asleep with his head on his arm
resting on the table.*]

> [*Three or four girls sing a stanza or two of some
> temperance song—very softly—from some con-
> cealed place on the stage. During the singing,
> enter Totie, a fairy, dressed in white, with a
> wand in her hand.*]

TOTIE [*looks at the sleeper*].—Ah! who have we here? This man needs my attention. [*Takes up the glass and looks at it.*] Oh! poor deluded mortal, why will you drink this vile stuff? I must help him to see his condition. [*Waves her wand over him. He starts up and looks around, wildly.*]

PENN.—Who—who—was that? [*Starts back with astonishment when he sees Totie.*] Who are you?

TOTIE.—Totie!

PENN.—Who?

TOTIE.—Te—to—tal. Totie for short.

PENN.—What do you want here, and with me?

TOTIE.—I came on an errand of mercy to you.

PENN.—To me? Well, now, that's a fine joke. Well, before you commence business, won't you have a little nip to waken up your spirits? Hey?

TOTIE.—No, I come to warn you. That [*pointing to glass*] is what demons feed fools and dupes upon.

PENN. [*aside*].—Demons again? [*Aloud.*] Fools and dupes?

TOTIE.—James Pennington are you a fool or a dupe?

PENN.—I acknowledge being a fool or a dupe? No! no, indeed!

TOTIE.—What is in that glass?

PENN.—Whisky; and good whisky, too, if I am a judge.

TOTIE.—What else?

PENN. [*looking in the glass*].—Nothing else there, Totie.

TOTIE.—You are blind, James Pennington. There is in that glass enough to make you cry out in despair and hide your eyes for very horror! There are demons in that glass.

PENN. [*starting*].—Demons?

[*Totie waves her wand—Disease appears.*]

PENN.—Who are you?

DISEASE [*in a hollow tone*].—My name is Disease. I am the messenger of Death, come to warn you. My home is there [*pointing to glass*], in the bottom of that cup.

PENN.—Rather a small home for you, I should think, from your size.

DISEASE.—It is large enough for me and all who are with me there. [*Exit.*]

[*Totie waves her wand—Poverty appears.*]

POVERTY.—My name is Poverty.

PENN.—I should say you are well named by your appearance.

POVERTY.—In the bottom of that glass is my home.

PENN.—I have never seen you there.

POVERTY.—You were blind. Thousands and thousands have found me there, as you will in reality at no distant day. [*Exit.*]

TOTIE.—There are others at the bottom of that cup Shall you see them?

PENN.—Oh no! no! I've seen enough! I've seen enough!

TOTIE.—But you *shall* see them.

[*Waves her wand and Crime appears, clad in rags, and chains on his hands and feet.*]

PENN.—I wish to see no more. This is horrible!

CRIME.—My name is Crime. I live at the bottom of yonder glass. By-and-by you will know me better, and do my bidding. I am a "Demon of the Glass." Those who use the glass, obey its lord.

PENN.—Oh! leave me! leave me! What does all this mean?

TOTIE.—There is more misery there [*pointing to the glass*]—you shall see more.

PENN.—I've seen too much now! My whole soul is full of terror. [*Fairy waves her wand—Poverty re-enters, bringing with him Edith and little child.*] Oh! merciful heavens! what do I see? Is it possible? That miserable woman, Edith? Edith Graham?

TOTIE.—This is a vision of the future. That is Edith, your wife, and that is your child.

PENN.—That my wife! That half-starved child mine! Oh, no! no! That can never be.

TOTIE.—Listen!

CHILD [*looking up at Edith*].—Oh, mamma, I am so cold, so hungry.

EDITH [*weeping*].—I know you are, my child, but food, nor clothing, nor shelter, I have not for you.

CHILD.—Will papa come for us to-night? I'm sure when he comes we will be happy again.

EDITH.—Alas! my child, your father fills a drunkard's grave, and we are left to starve. Once we were rich, but now all is gone. Misery, and only misery, is our portion.

> [*Pennington covers his face with his hands, and lays his head upon the table. A few stanzas of a temperance song are again sung softly by the girls, concealed on the stage. The fairy, Edith, etc., all exit, softly. * * * Stands up—looks around*]

PENN.—Was that all a dream? Oh, what a dream! [*Rings the bell. Enter Tom.*] Tom, take that glass away. There are legions of demons in the bottom of it—and bring me the COLD WATER PLEDGE. My resolution is taken. Never shall another drop of that vile liquor pollute my lips. That dream has saved me.

[*Curtain falls.*]

THE TWELVE MONTHS.
[FOR TWELVE LADIES.]
COSTUMES.

JANUARY, white dress with dark sash.
FEBRUARY, white dress with dark sash.
MARCH, same as February.
APRIL, white dress with green sash.
MAY, same as April, with a few flowers in her hair.
JUNE, same as May.
JULY, white dress with pink or red sash.
AUGUST, same as July.
SEPTEMBER, white dress with yellow sash.
OCTOBER, same as September.
NOVEMBER, white dress with dark sash.
DECEMBER, same as November.

[Each speaker should enter separately, and after speaking take her place in such position that after all have entered they will form a semicircle, facing the audience.]

JANUARY.—I come mid frost and snow to usher in the New Year. People dread me, and say that I am cold-hearted and stern; and it may be so, but I robe the ground with a mantle of fleecy snow, and I bind the babbling brook with fetters of ice. Although manhood and age shiver and tremble when I am near, yet the merry laughing children love me, and call me glorious January.

FEBRUARY.—My name is February. The month I represent, gave birth to a *Washington*, whose deeds of noble valor and heroism have caused me to be loved by all mankind, despite the cold and frost that still linger about me, bequeathed to me by my scarcely more stern and elder sister, January.

MARCH.—They call me March. My fiery and tempestuous disposition has led man to name me after the fiery little war-god, Mars. Yet, withal, I possess some redeeming traits of character. I melt the frost and snow brought upon the earth by my two elder sisters; I release the brooks from their icy fetters, and send them on rejoicing and babbling my praise. I am the harbinger of *Spring*.

APRIL.—It is said that I am unstable in character, and changeable; that I bring rain and snow, frost and thaw, alternately; but I labor for the good of mankind. I revive the earth; I unfold the green leaf, and I form the bud that is to unfold its petals and be perfected into a flower. Who shall say that April does not fulfill her appointed mission?

MAY.—I am called loving, laughing May. I expand the buds, and perfect the early flowers; (the buds of which my sister's hand fashioned.) I call the happy birds from the sunny south, and cause them to pour forth strains of sweetest melody to charm the ears of careworn man. The children love me, and call me their own dear merry month of May.

JUNE.—I come to herald the approach of Summer. I spread a carpet of beautiful green over the valleys, adorn the mountain tops with lovely flowers of the perfume and choicest hues. I strew the meadows with lilies and buttercups, and breathe soft warm zephyrs that ripple the smooth surface of the glassy lake, and bend the tops of the waving grass. Who shall say that the mission of June has been in vain?

SCHOOLDAY DIALOGUES.

July.—I am named after Rome's greatest **Emperor** Julius Cæsar. The month I represent gave birth to a nation of heroes and freemen. America claims me as her own, for, on one of my days, the great American Republic was born. The American people will never forget me; for, until the end of time, the *Fourth of July* will never cease to be hailed with pride and joy.

August.—I, too, am named after one of Rome's greatest Emperors, Augustus Cæsar. The month I represent, although perhaps it can not boast of containing the birth-day of a nation, yet I claim a high and noble mission. It is my mission to ripen the golden grain, and to prepare the harvest for the sickle of the reaper. Yes, the farmer loves August, for I bid him gather into his garner the products of his toil.

September.—It is my mission to finish what my sister began. I fold the petals of the flowers, and, breathing my cool breath over them, bid them wither and fade. I paint the forests with gorgeous colors of red, yellow, and green. I ripen the luscious fruit, and stain with delicate tints the rosy cheeks of the peach and apple. The golden corn I ripen for the husbandman. Ah, yes! September, too, has her mission of usefulness.

October.—It is my province to dismantle the earth of its robes of verdure. The delicate flowers wither and droop and die when they see me come. The little birds gather themselves into flocks, and flee away to a warmer clime at my approach. I breathe my cold chilling breath over the forests, and the leaves turn brown and sere and fall tumbling to the ground. October, too, has its mission, but alas! it is one of death.

November.—I come forth to behold the ruin wrought by my sister, and behold! all, all is dead! The brown, sere leaves lie scattered here and there, or are whirled about by the chill Autumn winds. Mankind call me cold and unfeeling November, and hail me as the dread harbinger of frost and snow; but such is my mission, and as such it must be fulfilled.

December.—Hail, sisters! I come to complete the circle of months. Mankind have branded me dark and gloomy December, and such I may be; for sleet and snow and cold frosty winds herald my approach. Men shiver and crouch beside their hearthstones where the fire glows brightly, when they hear my name pronounced; but the month I represent contains the birthday of the Saviour of the world. My mission is one of peace; then, though mankind shall alternately bless and curse us, still gentle sisters, let us join hands, and be at peace, and each perform her own allotted mission cheerfully and in love.

[*All join hands and sing.*]

> Let loving friendship join our hearts
> In peace and love sincere;
> Thus, while we each perform our parts,
> Shall pass the rolling year.

[*Curtain falls.*]

THE NEW PREACHER.

CHARACTERS.

Twister.	Fairman.
Wink.	Gimblet.
Bombasterson.	Coppermouth.
Highlook.	Blunt.
Twaddle.	Chub.

Worldly, and others.

Scene 1—*Neighbors lounging about the door of a country church after service.*

Twister.—Well, neighbor Wink, I observed you kept one eye on the preacher purty keen, this mornin'; what do you think of him, any way?

Wink.—Why, the fact is, if I was to say, that is, if I was to mention my 'pinion, so to speak, I can't 'xactly say that the sarmint pleased me. Just 'tween you and I, and I've hearn 'nough preachin' to know, he wa'nt altogether what might have been expected. Takin every thing into the 'count I must say that I was disappinted in the man.

TWISTER.—That's just what I was going to say myself, Mr. Wink, but I thought I'd like to hear your opinion first, for you are one of the sort of folks that don't hesitate to say whatever you think. Now, Mr. Bombasterson, what's your opinion?

BOMBASTERSON, [*in a deep, pompous tone*].—Hem! a-hem! As for me, I think the young man might do to *talk* on a small scale to some school-house congregation but as to *preachin'*, why, that isn't in him! He couldn't have been heered ten rod from the church, and his Bible lesson sounded more like talkin' than readin'. I like to hear a man fire up and steam ahead from the text to the amen, as if he had—a—a—hem!—as if he had——

FAIRMAN.—Lungs like an ox, Mr. Bombasterson? That is not my idea of eloquence. You have paid the new preacher an unintentional compliment, by saying his preaching and reading were like talking. I am glad we now have the prospect of hearing a man who has evidently studied the art of delivery, and has learned how to be natural in the pulpit, where, above every other place in the world, we should expect honesty of heart and naturalness of voice.

COPPERMOUTH.—I don't object to his manner so much as his matter. I'd like to know what right a minister has to preach in favor of war, and to pray for the success of armies of aggression against our southern brethren! I want to hear the pure Gospel when I go to church, and not politics. It's awful the way the pulpit has corrupted the people. I believe secession's a divine institution——

BLUNT.—So is the bottomless pit a divine institution! I glory in the Gospel that proclaims liberty to the captive, and loyalty to the Constitution, and I glory in the minister that dares to declare the whole counsel of God! I pray for the coming of the day when every Christian shall learn the blessed brotherhood of love as taught in the New Testament, and exemplified by our Union of States, and freedom of worship. Go home, Mr. Coppermouth, and read the Thirteenth Chapter of Romans, and if you can't indorse that, then go to the Confederacy at once, you traitor, and hear the mock Gospel that wil better suit you.

TWISTER.— Come, brother Blunt, you know the saying Blessed are the peace-makers"——

BLUNT.—Then blessed be our cannon, our swords, and our bayonets——

TWISTER.—Oh, you altogether misunderstand me!— I'm loyal sir, to our country, loyal, sir, but——

BLUNT.—Loyalty admits of no "buts" or "if's," sir. Your whole heart—your whole devotion, or nothing.

TWISTER.—You misunderstand me, brother Blunt—I only spoke of making peace between you and neighbor Coppermouth, for I'm afeard you are both a *l-e-e-t-l-e* excited.

BLUNT.—Well, perhaps so; for better men than either of us have been excited since this war began.

TWISTER.—Say, friend Highlook, you are a man of taste; what do you think of the new preacher? Will he do?

HIGHLOOK [*stroking his moustache, and twirling his cane*].—Will he do? Well, that is a mattah of gweat impawtance. The refawmation of our society at lawge depends upon the capacity of the ministah, to no inconsidawable extent. I was much mawtified to behold his black cwavat, and also to witness him wipe the perspiwation in the pulpit with a howid wed bandanna. To suit us, ow ministah must weah black gloves, white socks, and a white neck-tie, and use invawiably a white pocket handkerchief. Fawthamoah, his hair is a shade too light, and his eyes a little too keen for a placid ministah of the Gospel. I shall twy, howevah, to be satisfied, and to attend occassionally, when the weathah is faih, upon his ministwations, to encouwage the young man Good mawning, gentleman. [*He bows and retires.*]

TWADDLE.—I wish Mr. Highlook had studied for the ministry. I do like his beautiful address. And what good sense and elegant manners! What a pity that such splendid talent should not be used by the church! I would give a handsome sum to secure the services of a preacher that we could be proud of.

CHUB.—Raither perticler, friend Twaddle. For my part, I don't believe in eddycaten fellers to the preachin' business. The airly apostles was picked up from their fishin' seines, and sot right to work without any bookarnin' or polishin', and they was first-rate preachers, so they was. I'm in favor of none of your college-bred chaps, pretendin' to know every thing, and don't know how to turn a furrer or split a rail, so they don't.

FAIRMAN.—Gentlemen, it would take more than an angel, and less than a baboon to suit all of you.

WORLDLY.—He preached up too much piety for me For one, I don't calculate to sit still and be twitted of my sins every Sunday, and pay him for doin' it into the bargain. I left the house before he was more'n half done, just to let him see he daren't pitch into me.

TWADDLE.—I heered Mr. Highlook say he heered a man say, who heered this young minister preach somewhere once, that the people thought his sermon lacked depth.

[*Re-enter Mr. Highlook.*]

HIGHLOOK.—Excuse me, gentlemen, but I fawgot to say to you pwiah to my depawture, that it is to be feahed ow young ministah lacks depth of mind, if we are to judge from what the people say elsewhere, where he has held fowth. I undahstand, fawthawmoah, that his discoahses have no impwessive wohds whatevah, such as Jewawboam, the son of Nebat, Nebucadnezzah, Deutewonomy, Ecclesiasticus, or any of the ancient patwiarchs.

BLUNT.—Mr. Highlook, let me repeat to you for your edification a few lines:

"Oh, that the mischief-making crew
Were all reduced to one or two,
And they were painted red or blue,
That every one might know them."

HIGHLOOK [*highly offended*].—I shall see you again, sir! [*Withdraws.*]

BLUNT [*calling after him*].—If you do, you may hear the rest of that stanza. [*Aside.*] I do get indignant, sometimes, at the indiscriminate criticisms on preachers and preaching. [*One by one the company goes away, until all are gone but Blunt and Gimblet.*] Attend what church you may, you will hear, after the service, especially in the parlor circle where neighbors visit on the Sabbath, all sorts of unwarrantable opinions about the manner of preaching, and precious little about the subject matter of the discourse, and nothing, whatever, as a personal self-application of the truth. But I must be patient, and do *my* duty.

[*Starts toward home, when Gimblet, a silly, sponging fellow, follows him.*]

GIMBLET.—Say, Mister Blunt, I guess I'll go and take dinner with you to-day—'tisn't *much* out of my way. [*Exeunt.*]

THE SEASONS.

SCENE 2. *To be represented by fifteen girls, and one boy to represent* MARCH. *Each season with its months passes along, with appropriate fruits, flowers. grain etc.*

WINTER.

I COME from the distant frozen zones,
Where the ice ever binds, and the wind ever moans.
Cold, chilling winds follow fast in my track;
All frown at my coming, and wish me back.
The meadows I'll cover with a mantle of snow,
Which I scatter abroad wherever I go.
With ice I will silence the murmuring streams;
With clouds I will hide the sun's powerless beams.
All nature must sleep in my chilling embrace
Till the arrival of Spring, when I must give place.
My children are with me, my designs to fulfill,
They may speak for themselves; they all do my will.

DECEMBER.

I am the first-born of winter, yet of months am the last
All rejoice at my coming, yet joy when I'm past;
For my dark, gloomy days, and long, cheerless nights
Are illumined by naught save the gay Christmas sights
I am the favorite of the girls and the boys,
For with me come visions of Santa Claus' toys.
'Christmas is coming," and then you will hear
The last dying knell of the fast passing year.
Pause, now, and think what account it will bear.
But my mission is ended, my farewell's soon said,
And I hasten to join the years that are fled

JANUARY.

I am proud January, the first of the year;
All rejoice at my coming, and joy when I'm here.
Gladness and mirth follow close in my train,
"A happy New Year" is heard again and again.
My visions are bright, no forebodings I know;
My hopes tinge all objects with fancy's bright glow
Fondly I linger, still longer I'd dwell,
But I, too, must hasten to bid you farewell.

FEBRUARY.

As I am the *third*, and my days being few,
With not many words I will now trouble you.
I am short, cold, and crusty, I very well know,
But once in four years I kindly bestow
"A Leap Year," that ladies their husbands may choose,
Yet I give the *poor gents* a chance to refuse.
But I, too, must hasten away from your sight,
So to all I will bid " good night! good night!"

CHORUS.

We are passing away, but ere we are gone
You will hear the shrill notes of our winter song.

SPRING.

I come, the timid and gentle Spring,
Sweet treasures of beauty and blossoms to bring.
The streams I'll unlock from their fetters strong,
And soon you will hear them murmuring along.
The cold, chilling winds will vanish away,
For they know of my coming and will not stay.
All nature rejoices, for soon will be seen
The earth enrobed in its vesture of green;
And beautiful flowers springing every where,
Teaching a lesson of God's provident care.
From its distant home I call to the bird,
And soon will its joyous song be heard.
To the poor and the needy sweet comfort I bring,
And all rejoice to welcome the Spring.
But my children are waiting their gifts to bestow,
And we'll sing you a song as away we go.

MARCH.

I am bold March, the noisy, and proud;
Blowing my trumpet so long and so loud.
Fitful and stormy, a pest and a joy,
For all pronounce me "a troublesome boy;"
I care for nobody, no, not I,
So I'll take my leave without a "good-by."

APRIL.

Timidly I come as my rude brother leaves;
His boisterous manner my spirit oft grieves;
He chills my fond heart, and fills it with pain,
That my heart's dearest treasures I can not retain.
So I weep sad tears o'er the springing flowers,
And thus sadly vanish poor April's hours.

MAY.

Charming and gay comes the laughing May,
Singing and skipping the glad hours away.
Blooming so sweet are my beautiful flowers,
Decking with gladness earth's loveliest bowers.
The forests are ringing with music most sweet,
Happiest voices our ears ever greet.
How charming and gay around is each scene,
Clad in its garb of beautiful green!
With smiles and with joy I now pass away,
Leaving bright visions of blooming May.

CHORUS.

Brother and sisters, we pass along,
And sing, as we go, our welcome song.

SUMMER.

I come from a far distant Southern clime,
Where the orange-flowers bloom and myrtles twine;
Where the skies ever smile over glittering seas,
And richest perfumes are borne on each breeze.
To the North I come with my heated breath,
Bringing, too often, disease and death;
Yet in my steps comes the rich golden grain,
Luscious fruits I give you, they come in my train.

The year's bright noon-time, how pleasant it seems,
E'en under the sun's hot, scorching beams
My children, hasten and bring your store,
Gladdening the hearts of men once more.

JUNE.

I am June, and gladly I bring to you
Mild, balmy air, and skies of blue;
Days of soft and hallowed light,
Followed by a fairy, gentle night.
Long, long days of sunniest noon,
Mark the hours of radiant June.

JULY.

I am July, and close in my train
Come the rich harvests of golden grain;
Berries and fruits I will bring to you
Ere I pass away and say, "Adieu."

AUGUST.

August comes with its sultry days,
Bringing rich crops of the golden maize;
Yet causing all to sigh for the breeze,
Which only is found by the murmuring seas.
The city's deserted, all flee to green fields,
To taste of the joys which the country now yields
But my long tedious days at length will be done,
And I, like my sisters, must be passing along.

CHORUS.

Warm-hearted sisters for ever we be,
So sing, as we go, a farewell glee.

AUTUMN.

I come, grave Autumn, proud boasters to show
That their haughtiest works will soon be laid low.
I breathe o'er the forests, how changed they appear!
The grass withers away as if in sadness and fear.
I scatter the leaves from the loftiest trees,
And gather them up with the eddying breeze.

The songsters that warble so happy and gay,
All hasten to flee, at my coming, away;
Yet there's joy in my presence, for gladly I give
Of my richest abundance that mankind may live.
My children are weary with the burdens they bear
Of the rich, luscious fruits of the fast passing year.

SEPTEMBER.

Quiet comes the mild September,
Bringing joys that all remember;
Gladdening hearts with plenteous store,
That for all there's plenty more
Fruit and food; so none need fear
Want will trouble us this year.

OCTOBER.

Cool October greets you here,
With frosty breath, so pure and clear.
With its days, so calm and pleasant,
Will return the jay and pheasant.
Dropping nuts fall thick apace,
Gladdening many an urchin's face.
But my sunshine must give way
Before my sister's gloomy day.

NOVEMBER.

They call me "dull," and full well do I know
I can boast but of little save of rain and snow.
November's my name, which none will admire,
But shrink at my coming and call for a fire.
So quickly I'll leave, for I will not remain
Where my presence brings naught but sadness and pain

CHORUS.

Sisters are we of the fading year,
Please give us a song, our journey to cheer.

"LITTLE ANGELS."

CHARACTERS.

Mr. and Mrs. Brown, who reside in the country.
Mrs. Dosem.
Peter Jehosaphat Hezekiah Dosem.
Priscilla Aquilla Rebecca Dosem.
Adam Salathiel Dosem.
Rachel Abigail Dosem.
Ruth Sarah Dosem.
James St. John Simon Dosem.
Sisera Dosem.

Scene 1.—*Mrs. Brown, peeping from the window at the stage turning into the lane leading to her house.*

Mrs. Brown.—Good gracious me! What have I done to deserve such a judgment? If there hain't the Dosems a coming. I should know that green silk bun nit among a thousand, with them pink bows of ribbon onto it. Oh, deliver us! they've got that snapping poodle dog of theirn, and he'll scare the cat out of her seven senses. And only goodness knows how many children there is. I can count four heads stuck out of the winder. Dear, dear! what shall I do for dinner? I do wish folks would stay to home till they're invited.
[*Stage stops. Mrs. Dosem alights, bearing three band-boxes, a carpet-bag, an umbrella, and a huge bouquet, and closely followed by seven children—three boys and four girls. She throws down her burdens, and running up to Mrs. Brown, flings her arms around her neck.*]

Mrs. Dosem [*with empressment*].—Oh! Mrs. Brown! my dear, dearest Mrs. Brown! I declare it's been an age sense I last sot eyes on you! I told Mr. Dosem, day before yesterday morning, while he was eating breakfast—says I, "Mr. Dosem, I must leave every thing and go out to Lynnham, and see dear Mrs. Brown!" And Mr. Dosem, he said—"Most assuredly, Lucy." And he's gone out to board, and we've come—all of us! The children were wild to see their dear Aunty Brown once more—and they're such quiet little darlings I ventured to bring them! I knew you would be delighted to have them.

Mrs. B. [*faintly*].—Of course.

Mrs. D.—That's jest what I told Mr. Dosem, and he said, "most assuredly." Let me name them to you. It has been so long since you saw the darlings that you may, perhaps, have forgotten their names. Peter Jebosaphat Hezekiah, you are the oldest, come here and kiss dear Mrs. Brown.

Peter [*pulling the dog's tail*].—Don't see the pint!

Mrs. D.—The little angel! He's so witty. Dr. Pillwork said, when he was an infant, that he'd never live to grow up. He had too much intelligence of the brains to live. But I feel in hopes a merciful Providence will spare him to me. Adam Salathiel, you'll kiss Mrs. Brown, wont you, lammie?

Adam.—Shan't do it! Don't believe in kissing nobody but the "gals," and especially not folks with false teeth!

Mrs D.—Did you ever? Children will be children. Come, Priscilla Aquilla Rebecca—you see we took our children's names from the Bible. I do so dislike these novel-writer's names.

Peter.—Do dry up, marm, and let's go into the house; I'm hungry—I am; I want some sweet cake.

Mrs. B.—Yes, come in [*leading the way*].

Mrs. D.—I do hope your chambers are large and airy. It nearly kills me to sleep in a close, hot room. It affects my respitory apperatus so. Dr. Pillwork says I should have plenty of fresh air always.

Miss Priscilla [*an affected miss of fifteen*].—Are there any botanical specimens about here, Mrs. Brown?

Mrs. B. [*with a puzzled air*].—Well, I can't say. There may be, but there's never any of them been to this house I guess I hain't seed any.

Miss Priscilla [*aside*].—Heavens! what ignorance I shall perish among such savages.

Mrs. B.—Take off your things and set down, do.

Peter [*seats himself upon a table, which upsets, and he goes down with it*].—Golly, that's a turntable. Take your hoops out of the way, Sil, and give me a lift [*seats himself beside Priscilla on the sofa*].

PRISCILLA [*in dismay*].—Get up, instantly; you'll ruin my dress! Oh, dear me! what an infliction boys are—half-grown, uncivilized beings. Oh! ma, do make him behave. He's given my nerves such a shock. If I could only have a cup of tea at once.

MRS. D.—Mercy me! I hope you hain't going to have another of those nervous spells. Dear Mrs. Brown, I have an awful trial; Priscilla's nerves are so out of kilter, I have to be as particular with her as I would with an infant. Get the camfire, and a little cologne, and a fan. And do make a cup of tea just as quick as you can. I feel as if I should like a drop myself.

[*Exit Mrs. Brown.*]

MRS. D.—Mean, stingy old hunks! I never would have come nigh her, but she's got such a nice place out here, and she used to be a good cook. Children, you must stuff yourselves up well at dinner. Country air gives folks an appetite. We'll stay a month, if she only feeds us well. It will save us forty dollars a week.

MRS. B. [*entering, loaded down with bottles*].—Here's some camfire and arnica, and some essence of peppermint, but I hain't got no cologne.

PRISCILLA [*throwing up her hands hysterically*].—Good heavens! no cologne! How do people manage to exist?

[*Peter whistles Yankee Doodle, the two younger boys are playing horse, with the curtain-cord for reins, and the smaller girls pull hair behind the big rocking-chair.*]

MRS. D. [*perceiving them*].—My dearest Rachel Abigail, and my darling Ruth Sarah, what are you doing?

RUTH [*vindictively*].—She pulled my nose and made up a face at me. I'll cave her head in, I will.

ABIGAIL.—And she spit on my dress and scratched my face.

MRS. D.—Dear little lambs! they must have their innocent plays. James St. John Simon, take your feet out of Mrs. Brown's work-basket, my bird. Sisera, do be careful how you flourish that stick around that looking-glass. There! you've done it! Well, mind and not get any of the glass into your precious little feet. I'm real sorry it's broke, Mrs. Brown; it's such a bad sign. But, thank the Lord, it's only bad for the one that the glass belongs to.

PRISCILLA [*rousing up*].—Do send those dreadful children out to play. They'll kill me dead if they stay here!

MRS. D.—Yes, dears. Run right out and have a good ime. I suppose there's plenty of room about here?

MRS. B.—Do, please, children, be careful about tramping on the beans and cabbage plants. Mr. Brown is dreadful particular about his garden. There'd be an awful time if any thing should get pulled up.

MRS. D. [*indignantly*].—They wouldn't hurt a fly! Now, I guess Priscilla and I will take a little nap while you get dinner ready.

[*The children go scampering and screaming from the house, and Mrs. Brown shows Mrs. Dosem and Priscilla up-stairs.*]

SCENE 2.—*The dining-room. The Dosems seated at the table. Mrs. Brown, flushed and disconcerted, standing in waiting.*

MRS. DOSEM.—I see you have no coffee. I always take a cup of coffee with my dinner. The food relishes so much better. You needn't make it very strong And have plenty of cream.

PRISCILLA.—Pass me the bread, mother dear, if you please.

MRS. D.—My love, you must not eat any of that warm bread. It will injure your digestive organs. Mrs. Brown, have you any cold bread?

MRS. B.—No; I do not happen to have any.

MRS. D.—Indeed! I'm sorry. Good housekeepers are not often without cold bread. Well, just put this into cold water a minnit; only a minnit, remember Priscilla is so delicate.

RUTH [*vociferously, brandishing knife and fork*].— Give me some more sugar—enough of it. I want some with my bread and butter.

ABIGAIL.—And I, too! and some syrup! And give

me a piece of sweet cake! And I want a three-pronged fork.

JAMES.—Ma, Peter is eating up all the preserves; I shan't get a mite. Make him stop.

PRISCILLA [*languidly*].—Ma, I wish you would close that blind; the sun hurts my eyes. And do make Sisera stop drinking tea from her saucer. When will these children learn refinement?

MRS. D. [*suddenly*].—Where's Bounce? Here's just such a piece of steak as he likes. Where is he?

PETER.—In his skin.

MRS. D.—Don't be disrespectable, dear. What have you done with your sweet pet?

JAMES and ADAM [*together*].—He's in the well.

RUTH —He bit me for pulling his tail, and I hove him in.

MRS. D.—Good gracious! my darling in the well!

[*Enter Mr. Brown, in a state of angry excitement.*]

MR. BROWN.—What the deuce has been afoul of my garden? I'd like to know if there has been a drove of pigs along.

MRS. BROWN [*soothingly*].—My dear Solomon——

MR. B.—Don't "dear" me, Susan. I asked you what had been into the garden?

MRS. B.—My dear Solomon, don't you see there's company?

MR. B.—See! Yes, and hear, too. Will you answer my question?

MRS. B.—What has happened?

MR. B. [*furiously*].—You'd better ask what ain't happened. Somebody or other has tore all my beans up by the roots, and trod my potatoes into the ground, and tied my best rooster to the well pole.

PETER [*grinning*] —Golly! how he cackled!

MR. B. [*seizing the youngster by the collar*].—Did you do it? Speak, or I'll shake the breath out of ye.

PETER.—Lemme alone. Jim and I did it to see him squirm. Ruth and Nab pulled up the beans. Marm, make him let me alone. I can't git my breath. He's drunk, and smells of onions.

PRISCILLA [*falling back in her chair*]—Oh, heavens! I shall swoon.

Mrs B. [*excitedly*].—Oh, Solomon, dear! don't. Do let him alone. Don't, I beg, Solomon.

Mr. B.—You needn't beg, none of ye. I'm mad enough to shake you all to pieces. All my summer's work destroyed by a pack of young savages. If they belonged to me, I'd trounce every one of 'em till they couldn't tell 'tother from which.

Mrs. D.—Oh, my poor boy! There—he's tore Peter Hezekiah's collar. Good gracious! I wish we'd stayed to home.

Mr. B.—I wish to zounds you had.

Mrs. D.—I'll leave this instant. I hain't to be abused in this style. My angel children shan't be the victims of such a dreadful man. Where's my things?

Mr. B.—Here they are.

Mrs. B.—Solomon, I beg of you——

Mr. B.—It's no use, Susan; they shall leave. This woman did not know me last summer, when I called at her house just at dinner time, and now I don't know her. My horse is harnessed, Mrs. Dosem, and I shall be happy to take you to the hotel.

Mrs. D. [*indignantly*].—I wont ride a step.

Mr. B.—Walk, then. I'm willing.

Mrs. D. [*turning to Mrs. Brown, with dignity*].—Good-by, Mrs. Brown. I pity your condition with such a husband. I thank God that my angel children have not such a parient. Come, darlings, we will go. I will send for our baggage.

[*Exit the Dosems, en masse. Mr. Brown whistles the Rogue's March.*]

THE YOUNG STATESMAN.

Child.—Mamma, don't you think I would make a good statesman?

Mamma.—What makes you think so, my child?

C.—Why, phrenologists think I am gifted in the art of government and that I am bound to make a good lawyer

M.—Does it generally follow that good lawyers make good statesmen?

C.—Yes, as a general rule they do.

M.—But what are your own views of a good statesman?

C.—Well, mamma, I suppose a good statesman is one who understands the constitution of our country, is well versed in the history of our own and foreign nations, so that he can judge what is best suited to the wants of the people he represents.

M.—Are these all the qualifications that are necessary to make a good statesman?

C.—Well, he ought to be a good orator that he might be able to plead his cause in such a way as to excite the feelings, and awaken love, pity, or hatred, as best suited his subject.

M.—But are there no other qualifications of a higher order necessary?

C.—Oh, yes! he ought to have a good classical education.

M.—My boy, I do not depreciate the merits of a classical education, yet I do not think it absolutely necessary.

C.—Now, now, mamma, you are caught. Recollect how often you have told me that Moses was the greatest statesman the world ever saw, and you know "he was learned in all the wisdom of the Egyptians, and was mighty in words and in deeds."

M.—Very true, my boy; but was it his learning that made him such a great man?

C.—Well, mamma, I can only say with the inspired penman, that he was learned in all the wisdom of the Egyptians, and I suppose he wished us to understand that he was qualified for his office, and that it was learning that made him so.

M.—My beloved boy, the same inspired penman tells us he was not an orator. Aaron, his brother, had to be his spokesman; so you see his learning did not fully qualify him for his office.

C.—Then, mamma, it must have been his wisdom.

M.—But where did he get that wisdom?

C.—Why, mamma, you know he was educated in the court of King Pharoah.

M.—Ah, my boy! your last answer forces a sigh from the heart, and a tear from the eye of your beloved mother.

C.—Not for all the world would I bring a cloud over the sunshine of your happy face. You are all the world to me. What in my answer makes you look so grave?

M.—Oh, my beloved boy! I know you would not willingly grieve your mother, but—has her boy yet to learn that "the wisdom of this world is foolishness with God?"

C.—Then, mamma, you think the Egyptians were not wise.

M.—How could they be wise, when they knew not God; for the wisdom of this world without the knowledge of God makes a man so high-minded and so full of self, that he would break a world to pieces to make a stool to sit on.

C.—Mamma, where did he get his wisdom?

M.—Certainly not from his classical education, for the inspired penman tells us, that every good gift comes from above, "and that the fear of the Lord is the beginning of wisdom."

C.—Thank you, my own dear mamma; you have brought me to see that if a man is to be truly great, he must be truly good.

M.—Yes, my darling child, you have answered well at last.

C.—But where, mamma, in all the whole world will you find a man like Moses, who will stand up before a congress or parliament, and spread out his hands toward heaven, and speak and pray and plead with the Lord, as he did?—why the members of the house would say he was mad.

M.—Yes, my boy, they might even go as far as the Israelites did with Moses, when they were "commanded to stone him with stones."

C.—Oh, surely, mamma, they would not do so!

M.—I do not mean that in the nineteenth century any learned body of men would do so, but you know, my beloved boy, that hard words and cold looks fall as heavy upon a good man's heart as stones upon his flesh.

C.--Well, mamma, I see what you wish; is it not that every statesman should do like Moses? spread every *knotty question* before the Lord, and never, never to trust his own wisdom in order that he may be just and wise; and then, like Joseph, his words will have power and his way will prosper.

M.—Yes, my boy, you are now beginning to understand your mother's views of a "good statesman."

TWO WAYS OF LIFE.

SCENE, *a forest. An aged peasant is discovered, binding up a bundle of faggots. Enter a stranger, in a splendid military dress. He looks around as if bewildered, observes the woodsman, and speaks.*

STRANGER.—Good-evening, venerable father! will you direct me, of your courtesy, the nearest way to the castle of Königstein?

PEASANT [*who does not perceive the stranger*].—I must be going; little Eva will be on her way to meet me. [*He rises.*]

STRANGER.—I say! Good father! Are you deaf?

PEASANT.—I beg your pardon, my lord. Good-evening, my noble gentleman.

STRANGER.—Good-evening. Will you guide a belated traveler toward the castle of Königstein?

PEASANT.—The road lies beside the door of my cottage, and I am this moment going thither. Come with me, my lord, and if you will do us the pleasure to enter our humble dwelling, my Marie will be proud to offer you apples from our orchard, and the best of cheese and butter from her dairy.

STRANGER.—Thanks! And I, in return, will bestow this broad piece of *gold* upon your little Eva, as a keepsake.

PEASANT [*aside*].—He knows Eva's name. A gold eagle of the grand duke. [*Aloud.*] You must be very rich, my noble lord?

STRANGER.—Yes, my good friend; my cool head, and my good sword, *have* brought me wealth and honor And yet, *I* played beside a peasant's hut in *my* days of childhood, like your little Eva.

PEASANT.—And *now*, my honorable gentleman!

STRANGER.—And now.—The history of your country for the last ten years, is but the record of my deeds—I am the emperor!

PEASANT.—And what may that be, my gracious lord? It is, perhaps, one of the officers of the grand duke?

STRANGER.—Is it possible! And this is the *fame* I've fought and struggled for? No, old man! I am the *master* of the grand duke! Have you not heard that he has been driven from his dominions, and forced to take refuge in America?

PEASANT.—No, my lord; I had not heard of that. So the poor old duke is gone! He must be about my age I've heard my mother say, the joy-bells were ringing for his birth the morning I was christened. It must be a sad thing, to be driven from one's home and country in one's old age, my lord emperor!

STRANGER.—Yes. But we will not speak of that. What have *you* been doing these ten years past, not to have heard of these great events which have been going on around you?

PEASANT.—*I?* I have ploughed and sown the few acres my father left me; reaped and gathered in my scanty harvests. I have seen my fair daughter Lena grow up, in innocence and goodness, beside our humble hearth, and leave it, wearing the roses of a bride, to make the happiness of another not less humble. And since, I have seen her laid beneath the blossoms of our village graveyard, in the hope of the happy resurrection of the just. And now, *her* child—our little Eva—fills her place in our poor hut, and my good Marie guides *her* feet in the ways of obedience and truth.

STRANGER.—And have you been *happy* in this quiet life, old man?

PEASANT.—*Why not*, my lord emperor? I have a

cottage, dear as a lifetime's home can be. I have the society of my faithful wife, my patient, noble Marie; and we share between us the whole heart of our Eva—our winsome, prattling grandchild. I have a heart at peace with all mankind, and sure and precious hopes for the life which is to come.

STRANGER.—And such are the simple, homefelt joys my mad ambition has trampled upon! Josephine! now do I feel the justice of thy reproaches. [*Takes off his hat.*] My good friend, it seems you, too, have been a sort of conqueror?

PEASANT.—Why, yes, my lord. I have conquered some rocks and thorns in my rugged fields and gardens; and many a rocky fault and thorny grief in my own heart beside. But I thank my God, this hand has never been stained in the blood of a fellow-man!

STRANGER.—I wish *I* could say as much! [*Takes the hand of the woodsman.*] Old man, *the conqueror of Europe* ENVIES *your felicity!*

TOO GOOD TO ATTEND COMMON SCHOOL.

CHARACTERS.

TOM SMITH, a specimen of "Young America."
WILLIAM STEADY, } Schoolmates
CHARLES CANDID, }

TOM.—Halloo, Bill! which way so fast?

WILLIAM.—That is not my name, sir. My name is *William.*

TOM.—It seems to me that you are mighty particular. Well, *William*, then—*Master William*, if that suits you any better—which way are you walking so fast this morning?

WILLIAM.—Why, to school, to be sure, and I have but little time now to talk with you, for I fear I shall be late.

TOM.—Pshaw! what's the use in always being so

punctual, I'd like to know ? They don't pay you for it, do they?

WILLIAM.—I do not receive *money* from any one, if that is what you mean; but I *do* get well paid for being in season, by gaining the approbation of my teachers, and also by not losing any of my recitations.

TOM.—Perhaps *you* can, but *I* can not see that a fellow gains so much by worrying himself about being in school, always just to the minute. Why, one loses a good deal of fun in the street by that. Sometimes, just as the bell rings for school, the *fire bell* rings also, and then I like to run and see where the fire is, and how the machines work. You know, too, it might be our house, and then how bad I should feel not to be there. I think a boy might be excused for being a little late, at such a time.

WILLIAM.—I don't know about that, but I do know that running after engines is bad business for boys. They are apt to get into bad company, and hear bad language, and learn bad manners in such places. Then, too, they are apt to get in the way, and get hurt.

TOM.—Oh! that's all nonsense. The bad talk and bad manners don't hurt me; and as to getting in the way, I have helped to put out a good many fires. I can help draw a machine, and work it, too. Why, some of us boys "stole a march" on the engine company the other night, got out the machine, and worked it all by ourselves.

WILLIAM.—I grant you are rather smart—*Swift* by name, and *swift* by nature; but you will not convince me that the influence of such places and company is not already working in your mind for ill. I can see it in your talk now. This running about the street, when you should be at school, every good and wise person will tell you is bad business. But come, you had better go to school now. I must go. [*Starts.*]

TOM.—Oh! hold on a bit—don't be in such a hurry There is time enough yet. I am a good runner, and if I start when I hear the clock begin to strike, I can get to my school in time.

WILLIAM.—You see I am not so *swift* as you are. I can not stay any longer. There comes my friend Charles

SCHOOLDAY DIALOGUES.

Candid—he has a vacation to-day. I must leave you to finish this argument with him.

[Exit William and enter Charles.]

CHARLES.—Good morning, Tom.

TOM.—Good morning, Charlie.

CHARLES.—I noticed you and William were having an earnest talk What was the subject?

TOM.—Oh, his hobby—*school* and *punctuality*.

CHARLES.—I hope you did not disagree with him on that.

TOM.—Yes, I did. I go for the largest liberty, yet I am an advocate for attending school when it suits my convenience. He thinks I am a little reprobate, just because I like to be free, and run with the fire engine sometimes, instead of being at school just to the minute every day. I expect he takes his seat just at nine o'clock, and looks as demure as a little priest, and thinks he is very good.

CHARLES.—Well, sir, do *you* expect to get to school this morning? If you do, I will not detain you.

TOM.—Oh, I'm in no hurry. I am going down to the depot, before I go to school, to see the trains come in Don't we boys have good times jumping on the cars, riding a little, and then jumping off again?

CHARLES.—As to that I can not say. I never tried it. I expect you will get your head or limbs broken yet.

TOM.—Pshaw! I am not afraid of that. I can jump like a streak of lightning. But I see by your eye you are not pleased with my talk. You look like a very clever chap. Where do *you* go to school?

CHARLES.—To the Union school.

TOM.—*Why*, that's a free school, is it not?

CHARLES.—Yes; what of that?

TOM.—*Mother* says she would not let *me* go to a free school *"for all the world."*

CHARLES.—Why?

TOM.—There are bad boys who go there. *She is too careful of my morals for that.*

CHARLES.—*Well, well!* I think she must have an eye to them, indeed, from the fruits which I see. I guess *you* need not be afraid of any you would be liable to meet there. There is, *now* and *then*, by the way, a bad boy who chances to get into a private school.

Tom.—So father says; and he groans not a little about being taxed so much for these free schools, and once in a while, when he gets out of patience about taxes, he says, " *Hang it!* I have a good mind to send Tom to a free school and gain something myself." But mother says, " *Why, Tom go to a free school! never!* 'twould ruin the precious darling for ever!" So father yields—puts a new quid into his mouth and walks off to the store.

Charles [*laughing*].—Well, Tom, you *are* a pretty smooth talker, but to be a little more serious, I want to go back again to our starting point.

Tom.—I must say I am tired of this—but let us have your creed and end it.

Charles.—Well, I fully believe that a tardy boy is in great danger of becoming a truant, and in the end likely to grow up a loafer, with a fair chance of promotion at an early age, from the street school to the penitentiary high school, and from that, perhaps, to one of the state colleges, vulgarly called "State's Prison." It will make little difference whether he start in a *free* or *select school*.

Tom [*excited*].—*You impudent fellow!* I have a great mind to thrash you.

Charles [*putting his hand on Tom's shoulder*].— Hold on—keep quiet. This may seem severe, but I speak as a friend. You may yet thank me for it. Promise me you will think seriously of this, and mend your ways, before it is too late.

Tom [*hesitatingly*].—Well, I do not know what to say—perhaps I will, but——here comes the ten o'clock train—I'm off—good-by.

Charles [*alone*].—Poor boy! I fear he is on the sure road to ruin.

FIRESIDE COLLOQUY.

LUCY.—How beautiful the world is! The green earth covered with flowers—the trees laden with rich blossoms—the blue sky—the bright water, and the golden sunshine. The world is, indeed, beautiful! and He who made it must be beautiful.

WILLIAM.—It is a happy world. Hark! how the merry birds sing, and the young lambs skip—see, how they gambol on the hillside. Even the trees wave, and the brooks ripple in gladness. The eagle, too, oh, how joyously he soars up to the glorious heavens! the bird of liberty, the bird of America.

LUCY.—Yes:—

> "His throne is on the mountain top;
> His fields the boundless air;
> And hoary peaks, that proudly prop
> The skies, his dwellings are."

WILLIAM.—It is a happy world; I see it and hear it all about me; nay, I *feel* it, here, in the glow, the eloquent glow of my own heart. He who made this great world must also be happy.

LUCY.—It *is* a great world. Look off to the mighty ocean, when the storm is upon it; to the huge mountain, when the thunder and the lightnings play over it; to the vast forest, the interminable waste, the sun, the moon, and the myriads of fair stars, countless as the sands upon the seashore. It is a great, a magnificent world, and He who made it—oh, He is the perfection of all loveliness, all goodness, all greatness, all gloriousness!

FRANK.—What is the shape of the world, or of the earth?

WILLIAM.—It is round, or nearly so; it is what is called an oblate spheroid, having about twenty-three miles greater diameter from East to West, than from North to South.

LUCY.—Yes; you know, Frank, our little geography says:—

"The world is round and like a ball,
  Seems swinging in the air;
A sky extends around it all,
  And stars are shining there."

FRANK.—The world round like a ball! do you believe that, mother?

MOTHER.—Yes; men called navigators, have sailed around the world in ships, and come to the same place hey started from—like a fly walking around an apple.

WILLIAM.—That is called circumnavigating.

LUCY.—That is a very long word; I suppose it was made so, because it is such a great distance around the world.

WILLIAM.—Lucy, can you *spell* the word, and properly divide the syllables and pronounce them as you go along?

LUCY.—Yes; I think I can.

WILLIAM.—Well, go on.

LUCY.—Cir-cum-nav-i-gate. Circumnavigate.

WILLIAM.—You are correct, Lucy.

JOHN.—How far is it around the world? it must be a great distance, I think, mother.

MOTHER.—It is said to be about twenty-five thousand miles: I believe, I am right, William, am I not?

WILLIAM.—Yes; and its diameter is about one third this distance, or about eight thousand miles.

JOHN.—What is that which you call *diameter*, William?

WILLIAM.—The distance straight *through*, from one side to the other; just as I run this knitting-needle through this apple—thus.

FRANK.—William, how does any person know how far it is *through* the earth? no one has ever went through to measure it, I guess.

WILLIAM.—True, Frank; no person has ever actually measured it; but there is a mathematical rule that will find the *diameter* of any thing circular in form, when you have the *circumference*.

LUCY.—What is that, William?

WILLIAM.—If the *circumference* of the earth is twenty-five thousand [25,000] miles, by dividing this distance by the tabular number 3.1416, will give the diameter; and if the *diameter* of any circle or sphere be *multiplied* by this number, it will give you the *circumference*.

LUCY.—Oh, yes! and they know the distance around the outside; and to divide this distance by three, or that other number you mentioned, will give the diameter.

WILLIAM.—Yes.

FRANK.—Why, William, can they measure distance on the great ocean?

WILLIAM.—Yes.

LUCY.—How far is it to England, or across the Atlantic ocean?

WILLIAM.—About three thousand [3000] miles.

LUCY.—And the Pacific ocean, how wide is it?

WILLIAM.—It is called ten thousand [10,000] miles.

FRANK.—How many oceans are there on the earth?

WILLIAM.—There is said to be five oceans; but more properly speaking there is but *one*, having different names applied to different portions: as Pacific, Atlantic, Indian, Arctic, and Antarctic.

FRANK.—Why, I suppose there must be nearly as much water as land—how is it, William?

WILLIAM.—A great deal more water than land three fourths of the globe is said to be water, and one fourth land.

FRANK.—You astonish me!

WILLIAM.—To think, too, of the *tides* of the ocean— how the water rises and falls, twice every twenty-four hours—the incomprehensibility of its inhabitants —the great leviathan, how he sports therein, and other interesting things connected with the ocean, the heavens, and the earth—often constrains me to think of David when he sings in the one hundred and third psalm—"Bless the Lord, oh, my soul: and all that is within me, bless his holy name." The ninety-sixth psalm likewise is very beautiful.

LUCY.—
"God moves in a mysterious way
 His wonders to perform;
He plants his footsteps in the sea,
 And rides upon the storm!"

WILLIAM.—Why, Lucy, you seem quite poetic this evening; by the way, it is said the verse or couplet you just now repeated, contains all the *parts* of speech, grammatically speaking, in the English language; but for my part I think there is *one* of the eight parts wanting.

LUCY.—What is that?

WILLIAM.—The interjection.

FRANK.—I wonder how many people there are in the world?

WILLIAM.—It is said there are one billion [1,000,000,000] persons in the world; all of which are comprised in only five distinct races, called the Caucasian or white race; the yellow or Mongolian; the black or African race; the brown or Malay, and the red or American race, called also aborigines.

FRANK.—Why, are not we of the *American* race? We *live* in America, and were *born* here, too.

WILLIAM.—No; our ancestors came from Europe; we are sometimes called Anglo-Saxon, too. Our forefathers landed at Plymouth, in Massachusetts; a settlement was also made at Jamestown, in Virginia; but those settlements were made long after Christopher Columbus discovered America. You will observe, Frank, that the negroes born here in America are still called *Africans*, although they first saw the light and have been reared here in this country; and it would be the same were the Indians to go to Europe; they would still be called *Indians*, or "red men."

FRANK.—Were the Indians and negroes here in America when Columbus discovered it?

WILLIAM.—The Indian was, but not the negro; he was brought here by the English when they settled at Jamestown, and made a slave of by them; he was brought here from Africa.

LUCY.—I have often thought that the discovery of America, by Columbus, was in its effect, one of the greatest events that ever occurred in the world's history.

WILLIAM.—Most unquestionably one of the greatest events that has occurred, since the advent of our Saviour Jesus Christ into our world, has been the discovery of the Western Continent—great in a variety of ways; prominent among which is the GREAT GOODNESS OF GOD in opening a way or outlet, for the people of the over-populated countries of the Eastern Hemisphere; a land, too, where monarchy and despotism in the affairs of government find no favor. To think, too, what would have been the condition of millions of people, now happy, prosperous and contented, and in this glorious land of freedom—"the land of the free and the home of the brave"—if the great discovery of this continent had not then or since taken place But thanks to God for the realization of this sublime fact

Another great fact, scarcely less grand and stupendous, connected with the discovery of America, was the *demonstration* (of theory only heretofore) that the world or earth was round, or of globular shape. This proof has been of inestimable value to science and art; truly, astronomy and geography without this knowledge would be but a myth, and the celestial as well as the terrestrial world, an unknown and undiscoverable mystery. Oh! when I think, were it possible to obliterate all the attending circumstances, grandeur, goodness, greatness, and glory connected with this great event, "I am lost in wonder, love, and praise!"

FRANK.—When did Columbus discover America?

LUCY.—In the year one thousand four hundred and ninety-two. Three hundred and seventy-four years ago.

WILLIAM.—Yes, and now we number thirty-seven States, and a population of over thirty-one millions in the United States alone; then there is South America, Mexico, British America, West India Islands, etc., not included in this account.

FRANK.—Oh, Lucy, don't you remember that beautiful poem that you recited on last examination day, called "Three Days in the Life of Columbus?"

WILLIAM.—I suppose he refers to that beautiful translation from Delavigne, Lucy. Won't you repeat a passage from it, and that will conclude our pleasant *chit-chat* for this evening?

LUCY.—
> But hush! he is dreaming!—a vail on tne main,
> At the distant horizon, is parted in twain,
> And now, on his dreaming eye,—rapturous sight!
> Fresh bursts the New World from the darkness of night.
> O, vision of glory! how dazzling it seems!
> How glistens the verdure! how sparkle the streams!
> How blue the far mountains! how glad the green isles!
> And the earth and the ocean, how dimpled with smiles,
> "Joy! joy!" cries Columbus, "this region is mine!"—
> Ah! not e'en its name, wondrous dreamer, is thine.

But lo! his dream changes;—a vision less bright,
Comes to darken and banish that scene of delight,
The gold seeking Spaniards, a merciless band,
Assail the meek natives, and ravage the land.
He sees the fair palace, the temple on fire,
And the peaceful Cazique 'mid their ashes expire;
He sees too,—O. saddest, O, mournfullest sight!—
The crucifix gleam in the thick of the fight.
More terrible far than the merciless steel,
Is the uplifted cross in the red hand of Zeal.

Again the dream changes, Columbus looks forth,
And a bright constellation, beholds in the North.
'Tis the herald of empire! a people appear,
Impatient of wrong and unconscious of fear!
They level the forest,—they ransack the seas,—
Each zone finds their canvas unfurled to the breeze.
"Hold!" tyranny cries; but their resolute breath
Sends back the reply, "Independence or death!"
The ploughshare they turn to a weapon of might,
And, defying all odds, they go forth to fight.
They have conquered! the people, with grateful acclaim,
Look to Washington's guidance, from Washington's
Behold Cincinnatus and Cato combined,   [fame;—
In his patriot heart and republican mind.
O, type of true manhood! What scepter or crown.
But fades in the light of thy simple renown?
And lo! by the side of the Hero, the Sage,
In freedom's behalf sets his mark on the age;
Whom science adoringly hails, while he wrings
The lightning from Heaven, the scepter from kings

At length, o'er Columbus slow consciousness breaks, —
"Land! land!" cry the sailors, "land! land,"—he awakes,
He runs,—yes! behold it!—it blesseth his sight,—
The land! O, dear spectacle! transport! delight!

POCAHONTAS.

SCENE.—*A group of half a dozen Indians, and Powhatan in the foreground, with a large club in his hand. Captain Smith bound, hands and feet, lying with his head upon two stones.*

POWHATAN [*raising his club*].—

Ugh! when the wolf strays in the snare,
  The hunter has his prey;
No more the wolf shall seek his lair,
  Or prowl the hunter's way.

[*With a scream, Pocahontas rushes before her father, weeping, and throws her arms about him. Powhatan drops his club, and regards her savagely.*]

POCAHONTAS.—
    Oh, father, set the white man free,
      Hold back the lifted blow!
    Let not the lightning scathe the tree
      The winds have pinioned low.

POWHATAN [*sternly*].—
    Begone! and get you to your mates,
      As birds flee from the storm;
    A squaw's weak hands are useless weights
      To check the warrior's arm!

POCAHONTAS [*clinging to his right arm*].—
    These hands have plumed thy eagle crest,
      And wrought thy tufted crown!
    The dove shall flutter at thy breast
      Until thou strike it down.

    My father, spare the white brave's life,—
      I cling thine arm to speak;
    My veins are with the same blood rife
      As that which paints thy cheek;—

    Oh, hear her plea! Thy daughter prays,
      And when the sachems smoke
    Around the council fire's bright blaze,
      Thine own decree revoke!

    This guiltless blood will taint the breeze
      That climbs its skyward path;
    How shall Powhatan then appease
      Our great Manitou's wrath?

POWHATAN.—
    The braves inclose the council fire,
      Its secrets are their own,
    You know not of Manitou's ire.
      What signs to squaws are shown?

POCAHONTAS [*vehemently*].—
    The signs that streak the cloud's black fold
      With livid, zig-zag fire,
    That make the Indian maiden bold
      To stand before her sire!

The signs that walk across the sky
 And through the sunset's gold,—
They say the pale-face shall not die,
 That I thine arm shall hold.

Powhatan hears the young squaw plead,
 Will he not grant her prayer?
Oh, sachem, give thy daughter heed,
 And spare the captive there!

POWHATAN.—
Powhatan's word is like the life
 Powhatan's body holds,
And I have sworn to sheathe my knife
 Among his scalp-skin's folds!

[*Pointing to Smith.*]

POCAHONTAS [*pointing upward*].—
The eyrie bird swoops down to prey
 Upon the tame hawk's head;
The white dove soars across his way—
 He tears her breast instead.

She kneels by Smith's side, and lays her head on his.

As unto him thou would'st have dealt,
 Deal unto me the like.
My scalp shall dangle at thy belt,
 And now, my father, strike!

POWHATAN [*moved*].—
The Eagle will not wet his beak
 In his own nestling's blood;
Powhatan hears his daughter speak,
 And what she says is good.

[*Regarding her proudly.*]
The Eagle's spirit lives in thee,
 Thou hast his dauntless eye!

[*To his attendants, haughtily.*]
Unbind and set the captive free,
 The pale-face shall not die!

[*He folds his arms while they unbind Captain Smith who kneels to kiss the princess's hand.*]

[*Curtain falls.*]

BEAUTY OF FACE AND BEAUTY OF SOUL; OR, WHAT I WOULD BE.

CHARACTERS.

JULIANA, a gay young girl.
CHRISTOPHER, Juliana's brother, who would be a wit.
MARY, would be a genius.
LIZZIE, a sedate young lady who strives to be, and to do good.

[All seated together on a veranda, the girls examining a print of Cleopatra, while the young man is engaged in reading.]

JULIANA [*still gazing on the picture*].—Queen of wondrous beauty! it's no marvel that kings and princes, priests and generals, bowed at her shrine, and were made captives to her fascinations. I would give all the world to be as beautiful.

CHRIS. [*without raising his eyes from his book*].—"Handsome is that handsome does," my fair sis.

JULIANA.—No one asked *you* to speak. Boys are always interfering; and then you need not say any thing, for you know you had much rather be seen in the street with handsome girls than homely ones.

CHRIS.—And for a very good reason, pretty one. Being a truly affectionate brother, I, of course, should prefer the society of such as would remind me of "The girl I left behind me," at home. Besides plain looking girls are more generally sensible. [*Winking to Lizzie.*] And sensible girls would not be seen walking with me.

JULIANA [*in an offended tone*].—Talk as much as you please about sense, I know, and *you* know, too, that beauty is more thought of than any thing else. The high and low, learned and illiterate, young and old, rich and poor, all bow to the sceptre of Beauty. Even King Solomon, the wisest man that ever ruled a kingdom, wrote a great deal on the subject.

CHRIS.—Ahem! so he did, little one. "Favor is deceitful, and beauty is vain; but a woman that feareth the Lord, *she shall be* praised," so said King—S-o-l-o-m-o-n.

JULIANA [*with spirit*].—I wish father would make you go out to work with Patrick; the house is no place for boys.

CHRIS. [*laughing*].—Just so, I thought, petite Nannie, so I came out here to sit and take the air. Besides, mother tells me, that "the society of intelligent and refined young ladies, improves a verdant lad more than any thing else," so I am trying its effect, and think I can perceive an improvement. But girls [*addressing Mary and Lizzie*], why don't you speak? The veranda is open for discussion.

JULIANA.—I suppose they're afraid of having you for an opponent. Of course, you would be. The phrenologist said: "you were always on the contrary side," and he spoke the truth then——

CHRIS. [*interrupting*].—If he didn't when he said your bump of vanity was plus seven.

JULIANA.—You don't give the girls any *chance* to speak. Come, Mary, please tell us what you would rather be; and Lizzie, too. I'll keep still, and as for Chris, *he's* improved so much, there'll be no danger of your being interrupted by him.

MARY [*laughing*].—We all know Lizzie delights in doing good more than any thing else, (wish I could say the same of myself,) but I thought it was generally known that genius was *my hobby*. I almost worship genius wherever found, and would give the best half of the world to be a genius of some kind—either a poet, artist, or a celebrated vocalist. Why, I've almost a holy reverence for every word Lord Bryon has uttered (despite his faults and follies). Then there's Charlotte Bronte, Kate Hayes, and our own Hatty Hosmer. [*A pause.*]

LIZZIE.—Yes, dear Mary, we need not go to the Old World for fine specimens of genius, while our glorious Whittier lives (Freedom's noblest poet), and he *will* live for evermore; for the good and true never die. Their influence is as lasting as time, their "thoughts that breathe, and words that burn" are immortal.

MARY.—That is true, Lizzie; Whittier's genius is a noble one. Then there is our own "Anna Dickinson," of whose talent virtues, and genius we may be justly proud, and in point of physical beauty I think she will not suffer in comparison with Egypt's vaunted queen.

JULIANA.—That's *just* what I say. Geniuses are always beautiful.

CHRIS. [*shutting his book and jumping up*].—If I may be allowed to speak——

MARY and LIZZIE [*speaking at once and laughing*].—Certainly, "the veranda is open to discussion."

CHRIS.—I presume you *all* accord to Dr. Watts great genius?

GIRLS [*in one breath*].—Yes, we do.

CHRIS.—And have heard the story about his physical deformity?

JULIANA.—No!

LIZZIE.—What is it?

MARY.—Please tell us.

CHRIS.—He was a small, plain-faced, illy-formed man, and, at one time, was in company, among whom were some strangers, and he was pointed out to one of them as "the author, Dr. Watts." When the stranger exclaimed, in astonishment, "What! that the great Dr. Watts! That little, insignificant man!" Whereat, the doctor drew himself up, and with upraised arms, repeated slowly and distinctly, these impromptu lines·

"Were I so tall as to reach the pole,
 And clasp the heavens with a span,
I must be measured by my soul,
 The *mind* is the standard of the man."

And that's what I call genuine wit.

LIZZIE.—Coupled with true greatness, Christopher.

JULIANA.—Yes; Chris. is always harping upon wit. Artemus Ward is his hero. [*Laughing.*]

CHRIS.—I never shall have for my heroine an *infamous woman*. Though she *be* as beautiful as an angel, I should know 'twas a "fallen one." [*With emphasis.*]

MARY.—We must give to every one his just due Cleopatra was talented and highly accomplished, as well as beautiful in person—and 'tis for that I admire her—her rare gifts of intellect. What say you, Lizzie, to that?

LIZZIE.—I am reminded at this moment, of words uttered by a little boy. He had heard read "Byron's

Address to the Ocean," when he turned to his mother, and said, "It is *grand*, it is *beautiful*, mother, but there's no God in it." And I would that all lovers of literature were as discerning in regard to the excellencies and defects of the authors they read, as was that little boy. There should be an evident aim to benefit, as well as to please the imagination of the reader; as a friend remarked the other evening upon the writings of T. S Arthur, that, "though there was a sameness in his stories, still she liked them, for he seemed to have an aim, and that was what she wanted to see in a writer." And I think it may be said of that excellent writer, as was said of one in former years, that "he never wrote one line which, when dying, he would wish to blot out." We should live to do good.

CHRIS.—You express my sentiments exactly, if I am a harum-scarum youth; but it's my *opinion* the more *wit* one possesseth, the more good he can accomplish.

MARY.—I indorse Lizzie's sentiments, too, and I don't know who *can* "do good," if a real genius can't But they're not always good.

JULIANA.—Well, I'm not going to give up beat, without *one* word more. What's the first question asked when a stranger's name is introduced? Isn't it "how does he look?" "is she, or he, handsome?" etc.

CHRIS.—With all due respect for the opinion of my sister, I must say no; who would ever think of asking if N. P. Willis and Professor Longfellow were pretty men [*in a depreciating tone*]? We all *know* they have beautiful souls, and Whittier says, the "Good are always beautiful." [I believe it is Whittier.] Mary must correct me if I'm wrong. [*Mary nods assent.*] I had *much rather* see a plain house *well furnished*, than to see a splendid structure unfurnished, or but poorly furnished. Who would want to stand out of doors all the time to look at the outside of a house? I should want to enter into the *inner sanctuary*, and find something on which to feast *my soul*. You see I'm getting sentimental [*humorously*]. Well, it's all the effects of the company I've been in, but [*looking at his watch*] the hour for my recitation is near, and I must leave, though with reluctance, for I'm convinced mother is about right in regard to her opinion of society. [*And wishing the girls a* VERY *pleasant afternoon, bows, and retires.*]

LIZZIE.—I think, Julie, you are not altogether in fault. We are *too apt* to inquire how a person looks. But I think it's more a habit we have fallen into, than a fixed principle, though we all like to see a fine face and form. But if there is not a corresponding beauty of mind and soul, we are sadly disappointed. There occurs to memory one, of whom I never heard the question asked, "how did she look?" 'Tis the sainted Mary Lyon; we each know of her self-sacrifice, devotion to her calling, and the *great* good she accomplished. And I am sure that *either of you* would rather have the same said of you, when you've passed away from earth, than that you were merely a great genius, or a celebrated beauty?

MARY.—Yes, Lizzie, I would.

JULIANA.—I suppose so, if there could be but *one thing* said of me.

LIZZIE.—"For the eye and cheek will fade,

MARY [*repeats*].—Beauty owns immortal grace;

LIZZIE.—Throned she sits within *the soul*,

MARY.—*That is beauty's dwelling-place.*"

LIZZIE.—Yes; the form so admired to-day for its comeliness, will in a few years decay and moulder in the dust; "but the soul, immortal as its sire——"

MARY and LIZZIE [*in concert*].—"*Shall never die.*"

LIZZIE.—Then, since all of earth must perish, may we each strive to possess what *never fades*—the beauty of the soul. [*Scene closes.*]

UNCLE ZEKE'S OPINION

CHARACTERS.

PROFESSOR.   TEACHER.   PATRIOT.   POET.
UNCLE ZEKE (an old fashioned farmer quite aged).
SETH SPRIGGINS, a Green Mountaineer.

UNCLE ZEKE. [*sitting apparently in deep reflection, commences talking*].—Well, I havn't got much longer to live, and I don't care. There's nothin' much worth livin' for in this world now, the way things is goin'. This country my father fought and bled and died for, on Bunker's Hill, is no longer the happy, harmonious republic they then established; but a great, over-grown, sickly thing, havin' within itself the elements of its own destruction. Ever since I heard the Charter Oak had fell, I have knowed its doom was sealed. Alas! it is droopin', witherin', dyin'. It is torn limb from limb by nternal factions; its best friends is its greatest enemies.

PATRIOT.—What is the matter, Uncle Zeke, that you should be letting off your superabundant steam in that fashion? You, one of our best men, the son of that brave little band that shed their blood so freely, and gave our nation the deathless name it then acquired; you, sir, to turn recreant to the principles they there defended; you, who stood by her in her adversity, to forsake her in her prosperity, when she stands the pride of the continent, the chief luminary of the world Nobly did her sons establish her name! nobly have *their* sons protected and improved their patrimony!

TEACHER.—Yes, nobly! and in what way more nobly than in designing and perfecting the admirable system of common schools we possess—the secret of our prosperity, the talisman of our success.

UNCLE ZEKE.—There you have it! Common schools Common humbugs! Instead of havin' schools to larn the boys readin', ritin' and siferin' and such like, that 'll be some good to 'em, they larn 'em nateral flosity and watermology and sintacks, and I don't know what kind o' nonsense, what is no manner o' use to 'em, 'cause nobody understands it but them college-bred milk-sops that come among honest people and pertend to teach, and then run away with the old folkses' money, and the boys' brains, and the gals' hearts, and then chuckle and shake their bony sides over their victories.

PROFESSOR.—How absurdly you talk, uncle! Every one admires our superior system of education; it is one of our great national institutions which have won for us a deathless reputation among the nations of the earth. Take away our common schools, and you deprive us of one of the richest blessings we enjoy;

the very life-blood of our prosperity; the principles for which our forefathers fought, and the sweet, rosy-cheeked maidens of seventy-six taxed their energies to secure.

SETH SPRIGGINS.—My Arcles! Maidens of seventy six! Well, if ever I heard wimmen as old as that called maidens afore! I wonder when yeou'd call 'em wimmen When 'Squire Dorgwood, from Orange county married old Sally Stubbs daown to Bennington, nobody called *her* a gal; every body called her an old woman, and she was only seventy-tew, that was [*counting his fingers*] four year younger than your maidens, tew. Her face was as wrinkled as a dried apple, and abeout as rosy.

PATRIOT.—Astonishing! Astonishing!! that one of our free and enlightened Americans, in '62 should not *revere* the very figures that express '76, saying nothing of the idea of failing to recognize the plain mention of an era rife with so many associations so dear, so thrilling, so exalting to every member of our glorious Union.

POET.—

Let her banners flutter proudly
  On every flagstaff, spire, and tower;
Let her statesmen discant loudly
  On her greatness, honor, power;
Let true hearts with ardor burning
  Strive her virtues to increase;
And while others war are learning
  Teach her children love and peace.

UNCLE ZEKE.—Sickenin' love pieces are plenty enough now, I calkelate. You can't take up a paper, nor book, nor nothin' without it's full of love pieces; and afore children is big enough to have nateral love feelins, they get their heads so full of this love-nonsense, they never have none of the nateral love feelins at all. The love them books tells about is no more like love than the hooped flyaways we see now-a-days is like the neat, pretty, slim, red-faced gals that I used to court when I was a young chap.

TEACHER.—Oh, Uncle! you are getting crazy. Thinking about your old courting days has bewildered you We are not speaking of love pieces, but of love *and* peace. Peace, freedom from war, rest; not pleas part.

UNCLE ZEKE.—Oh, dear, sus! That's all, is it?

TEACHER.—That's all. We know there is much trash published; but we can't stop that without suppressing profitable literature, also; and all we can do is to counteract its influence by diffusing morality, religion, and science.

PROFESSOR.—Morality and religion are the effective agents. Science, the root from which they derive their support. Science has dethroned heathenism in many ases. It is driving superstition before it, and will ventually prostrate it to rise no more. The lightning which our ancestors looked upon in dismay as it flashed from cloud to cloud, has been brought from its sublime throne, by the hand of science, and is now one of man's most useful and obedient servants. The vapor which arises from heated water, which, in olden times was looked upon only as a curiosity as it dashed the lid from the caldron in which it was boiling, is now the motive power that impels us across the ocean in splendid palaces, or hurls us over the country with electric speed. The planetary system, which was regarded with wonder and dread by the ancients, who worshiped its various members as deities, is now only a vast concourse of worlds rolling through the immensity of space Science has done all this, and yet you despise it. It is the centre of gravity around which our country revolves; the very essence of its existence.

UNCLE ZEKE.—I guess, old chap, you'll have to preach a longer sarmint than that afore you make this old child believe that 'are nonsense. With all your larnin' I don't believe you'll get one inch nearder the stars than I will, or stan' a flash of lightnin' a bit longer after it hits you.

PATRIOT.—That may all be so, uncle, but don't say any thing more against our Union. Let us rapidly review her progress since she came into existence. Then she consisted of thirteen little stars on her flag; now that cluster has multiplied and increased till a fiery constellation of thirty-seven blazes amid its silken folds, besides territories almost boundless that have no repre sentation there. Empires may crumble; kingdoms may fall; tyranny spring up, flourish its little hour, and then fall to the ground; but our republic must flourish and increase while time and space endure.

POET.—
Time shakes the stable tyranny of thrones.

SETH.—Who knows but it was time shook aour stable daown; I thought it was the wind.

TEACHER.—Not a horse stable, but the adjective stable, permanent, fixed.

SETH.—Ourn wasn't a hoss-stable nor an adjective stable nuther; it was the calf stable at the back end of the barn. There was three calves in it, and the red one got killed, and the spotted one got its head onjointed, and its tail smashed a-most off, so it died before we found it the next mornin'.

TEACHER.—I think there was one calf escaped that disastrous end, or you wouldn't be here to talk such nonsense.

SETH.—Oh, yes! The black one didn't get hurt a-bit.

PROFESSOR.—Such ignorance as this individual manifests is intolerable; unworthy the enlightenment of the present century.

SETH.—Ef I ain't worthy this censure, I can dew withaout it. I don't want yeou nor your censure nuther

TEACHER.—He isn't speaking of censuring you.

SETH [*angrily*].—He did say censurin', tew; I hearn him.

TEACHER.—You can say it means what you like: that's just the way.

PROFESSOR.—It is useless to attempt to convince the ignorant of any thing that is not perceptible to the senses; therefore——

UNCLE ZEKE.—Who can convince any body of any thing other than by their senses. If their senses isn't wantin' why can't you convince a dog or cat or a hoss of any thing as well as a man.

PROFESSOR.—By the senses we mean the faculties of hearing, seeing, smelling, etc.; not intellect.

UNCLE ZEKE.—I don't know what intelleck is; but I know neighbor Dobson's Bill could hear and see and smell as well as any body, and he hadn't no sense at all.

Professor.—I love to respect the aged where the case will admit at all : but this is too flagrant a violation of reason to allow respect or mildness; it is insufferable.

Poet.—

> Concealed within the marble block
>   The polished statue stands;
> Yet only issues from the rock
>   Beneath the sculptor's hands;
> Just so the mind, the living mind,
>   Hidden in darkness lay;
> No light burst from its powers, confined,
>   Till education cleared the way.

Seth.—Haow mighty knowin' you think you be! That rhymin' ain't nothin'. I can make better varses than them by a jug full. I know some a good 'eal better than that feller's.

Professor.—Please recite them.

Seth.—There ain't a sight of them; only tew.

Professor.—Say them then. Do you understand that?

Seth.—Yes, easy! Well, listen——

> I went daown to Cap'n Blake's
>   And there I seen his darter:
> I never seen a prettier gal,
>   Or one what acted smarter.
> Her eyes is like two lightnin' bugs,
>   Her lips like lemon candy;
> Her cheeks is like a robin's breast,
>   And ear-rings, aint they dandy?

Professor.—Well done! You seem to possess some faculties notwithstanding. Quite a poet.

Seth.—I don't know whether I've got any or not. I've got a good many things in my trunk; I guess there's some amongst 'em.

Professor.—What a paragon of ignorance; and yet that individual is under the influence of the tender passion, judging from his poetic effusions, and probably contemplates entering into matrimony.

Seth.—What sort of money?

Professor.—Yes I say you probably contemplate entering into matrimony.

SETH.—I daon't know exactly, but I guess I d take any thing that would pass. I wonder if a body'd let me have a chance to earn it.

TEACHER.—Were you ever at school, sir?

SETH.—Oh, yes! I went to school three afternoons, but the first the master wasn't there, and the next he was drunk, and the last he kept talkin' to Kate Robbins, and didn't larn us nothin'.

UNCLE ZEKE.—Well, I went to school a good 'eal when I was a boy. I went three winters day-times, and one, evenin', too; and I guess that *was* a school. There was no jimnastiums and excesses there; none of your new-fashioned fooleries. If the boys didn't behave, they got the ferrel; and if the gals didn't carry 'emselves straight, they had to stan' upon the bench till they felt cheap, I tell you.

TEACHER.—And that was the school system you admire. What branches did you learn?

UNCLE ZEKE.—We larned readin' and ritin' and siferin'; and that was plenty for common folks to know. Ministers ort to know a little more so as to expound the scriptures a little; but for boys to larn big words and high branches, and the gals to larn drawin, paintin', music, thumpin' the pianour, and pinchin' the guitar, instead of spinnin', weavin', nittin' stockings and makin' close, is the ruination of all of 'em ; and when the people is ruined, the nation is ruined, brag on it as you please.

PROFESSOR.—The use of machinery has superseded the old-fashioned spinning-wheel and hand loom ; *they* are only relics of by-gone days. The day is fast approaching when the buzz of the spinning-wheel, and the clatter of the loom shall be heard no more in our land for ever. The piano and guitar have taken their places. and our maidens may learn music, and our sons science, while steam performs the labor they formerly were obliged to do.

TEACHER.—The Lyceum is now about to go into session, gentlemen. Please step into the next room. *Exit all but Uncle Zeke.*]

UNCLE ZEKE.—Jes so, Mr. School-master, but if yeou'll wait *'ill I see em* in their precious mess of tomflumpery yeou'll wait till yeou're grayer than yeou neow be. [*Exit Uncle Zeke, calling to John to drive around the team. Noise, as if the old gentleman was climbing into an ox-cart, and the oxen restless.*]

THE SPELLING CLASS.

[This piece can be spoken by either sex, or by both, by changing names. A large boy or girl should be selected as teacher.]

PUPILS.

JOHN.	SAMUEL.	MICHAEL.
JAMES.	DANIEL.	JOSIAH.
WILLIAM.	JOSEPH.	CALEB.
PETER.	HENRY.	PATRICK.

SCENE 1.—*Pupils playing on the stage when the curtain rises.*

TEACHER.—Now, boys, I want you to form into a class, and spell the lesson I assigned you.

ALL THE BOYS.—Yes, ma'am.

TEACHER.—Peter, you may go to the head of the class this evening.

MICHAEL.—Teacher, Pat Flannigan's head. He trapped Jim Barnhill last evening.

CALEB.—No, Pat Flannigan's not head though; I'm head, I guess. I trapped Pat at the word conglomerate didn't I, Josie?

JOSIAH [*slowly*].—I don't know, I wasn't in school yesterday.

WILLIAM.—Teacher, I was third last evening, and now Joe Davis won't let me in my place.

TEACHER.—Joseph, let William in his place.

SCHOOLDAY DIALOGUES. 121

HENRY.—Well, I wasn't foot, either, when we spelt last, for I marked my number on this paper, and I was fourteenth. [*Holding up the paper.*]

TEACHER [*counting the class*].—Why, you are twelfth now, and last evening you say you were fourteenth.

HENRY.—Well, but I wasn't foot.

JOHN.—Please, ma'am, Dan Lutz is pinching me.

TEACHER.—Daniel, walk to the foot of the class.

PETER.—Teacher, shall I go head?

TEACHER.—Yes, I told you to go there when I called the class up, didn't I?

PETER.—Yes, ma'am.

CALEB [*as if crying*].—It's not fair. I was head.

TEACHER [*holding up a stick*].—Quiet, now, or you'll get a good flogging.

JAMES.—Please, teacher, Sam Snodgrass is standing on one foot.

TEACHER.—Samuel, stand erect. The class will all pay strict attention. Peter, where is the lesson for this evening?

PETER.—On page forty-nine, lesson fourth, section seventeenth.

JOSEPH.—John Barnhill told me, that we were to get the last section on page forty-eight.

SAMUEL.—And Dan Lutz told me that Bill Smith told him that we were to get the first two sections on page fifty. He said that Josie Lichtenberger heard the teacher say so.

TEACHER.—Did you hear me saying so, Josiah?

JOSIAH [*slowly*].—No, ma'am, I wasn't in school yesterday.

TEACHER.—Joseph Davis has the right place. He will go to the head of the class, and Peter may take his place at the other end of the class.

HENRY.—Why! I'll be ahead after awhile, if them fellers keeps coming down here much more.

TEACHER.—Quiet, there. Attention all. Joseph, spell the first word.

JOSEPH.—Teacher, I don't know what the first word is.

TEACHER.—Well, if you only have a little patience I will pronounce it for you.

CALEB [*hand up*].—I know what the first word is.

TEACHER.—You keep quiet, until you are called upon to speak. The first word is commutation. Spell, Joseph.

JOSEPH.—C-o-m, com, y-o-u, you, comyou,—

TEACHER.—Next.

WILLIAM [*drawling*].—C-o-m, com, m-u, mu, commu, t-a, ta, commuta, s-h-i-o-n, shun, commutation.

TEACHER.—William, you must get your lesson better the next time.

WILLIAM.—Please, ma'am, I have no book. Somebody stepped on it, and the skin came off.

TEACHER.—The cover, you mean, don't you?

WILLIAM.—No, ma'am, I mean the outside of the book, the skin.

TEACHER.—Well, what did you do with the inside of the book?

WILLIAM.—Why, it looked so ugly, that one evening last week, as I went home, I threw it into the creek down there.

TEACHER.—You deserve a good whipping; but we must continue the spelling. Patrick, you spell?

PATRICK.—Plase, mar'm and I don't know the w-u-r-r-d.

TEACHER.—James, spell.

JAMES.—C-o-m, com, m-u, mu, t-a, ta, t-i-o-n, tion, commutation.

TEACHER.—That is right; go up.

JAMES [*goes up and William trips him*].—Teacher, Bill Smith tried to throw me down.

TEACHER.—William, you will take your seat. John, do you spell the next word, molasses.

JOHN.—M-o, mo, [*smacks his lips*] m-o, mo, [*smacks them still louder*] m-o-l-e, mole [*still smacking.*]

TEACHER.—What is the matter?

JOHN.—I can't spell that word; it's too sweet.

TEACHER.—Josiah, you can spell it.

JOSIAH [*whose head has been turned in an opposite direction, now faces the teacher, and spells slowly*].—S-u, su, g-a-r, gar, sugar.

TEACHER.—That is not the word.

JOSIAH [*slowly*] —Why, John said it was so sweet he

SCHOOLDAY DIALOGUES. 123

could not possibly spell it, and I thought he meant sugar.

TEACHER.—I don't believe you are paying attention.

CALEB.—Teacher, I know how to spell the word.

TEACHER.—Spell it, then.

CALEB [*very earnest*].—C-a-n, can, d-y, dy, candy. [*He goes up.*]

TEACHER.—Hold on; that is not the word. Go back to your place. You all deserve to be punished severely for your neglect in preparing this lesson, and your indifference in the recitation. Let me hear you define a few words. Henry, what is the meaning of the word exterminate?

HENRY.—Exterminate, means that natural reflection subsiduary upon longitudinal molusc, when the conspicuous generality of ideas, encompass the plausibility consequent upon the gelatinous machinations of pneumatics, during the precise admonitions of an avaricious duadecagon: or, in other words, the incomprehensible gyrations of antiquated logarythms, when in a state of lubricating gymnastics, produced from the exhilarating effervescence of hydraulic aspirations, flowing from the ambiguous castigations in the colossal amphitheatre of redundant asseverations, while renewing the categorical receptacles of an ignited concatenation.

TEACHER.—Very well done, Henry; I am pleased to see that you studied the lesson so well.

MICHAEL.—Teacher, I don't exactly understand about that avaricious duodecagon.

TEACHER.—Henry, please explain those words for the satisfaction of the class.

HENRY.—Why, an avaricious duodecagon, simply means a black spotted cat with a long white tail.

TEACHER.—Now, Samuel, brighten up, and give me a short definition of the word procrastination.

SAMUEL.—Well, the literal meaning is systematically that phenomena of auxiliary conceptions, which by their egotistical perplexities affiliate with the aromatic plausibilities of an analytical stove-pipe, that has for its origin the unavoidable periphery by which it is metamorphosed into an exaggerated chrysalis of oleaginous invisibility

TEACHER.—That is excellent. I knew there was something in you, if only the right method was taken to extract it. The audience will readily see the importance of pupils being thoroughly conversant with language, so that they will be able at all times to disseminate that light among those around them, which should characterize the enlightened era in which we live Now, boys, we will close the lesson for the present, hoping that you are all more sensibly impressed with your duties. Continue in the course you have commenced, and you will become great men and *women*.

[*Boys leave in confusion.*]

THE TWO TEACHERS.

CHARACTERS.

CLARA, a faithful teacher, who loves the employment.

LIZZIE, one who dislikes teaching.

SCENE. *A School-room.* CLARA *stands by a desk reading, while a group of little ones are preparing to leave. Before they go, they take an affectionate leave of the Teacher.*

[LIZZIE *enters hastily, as if she had been walking a long distance.*]

CLARA [*starting forward*].—Why, good afternoon, Lizzie! Your school must have been out early; for now it is only half past four, and you teach four miles away. I expected you to-night, but not so soon.

LIZZIE.—I dismissed school a little after *three*. There! you needn't look so terrified! I guess the scholars

were glad enough to get away. I am sure I was!
Oh! it did seem so good to get out in the pure, fresh
air, away from the noise of the children. But come,
Clara, let us dismiss such dismal things as school,
scholars, and teaching, from our minds. Let us "drive
dull care away" with song. [*Taking a singing book
and sitting down*] Dear me, I'm so tired! I am glad
there's no school to-morrow! Let us sing, "Rain on
the Roof." You sing alto and I will soprano [*sounding
key*].

CLARA [*half impatiently*].—No, not now, Lizzie,
please; I want to talk a little while.

LIZZIE.—Well, my dear, I suppose you are going
to lecture me. Proceed! I'll bear all your good talk
with the patience of a martyr. [*Folding her hands
demurely.*]

CLARA [*soberly.*]—By what you said of your gladness to get from school, etc. etc., I am afraid [*hesi-
tating*]. To come to the point, Lizzie, do you like
to teach school?

[*The mischievous smile died out of Lizzie's face, as
she arose quickly and said in a hurried tone:*]

LIZZIE.—Like to teach school? What a question!
Clara, did you, could you, think I did? [*Speaking
slowly*] Ask the little bird, that carols its free, joyous
song on the tall tree, free to act at its own sweet will,
ask it if it likes its prison cage as well as its covert of
green leaves. Ask the babbling brook, which wends its
way, singing merrily as it goes, if when imprisoned in
the still pond, its poor, suffering heart does not long to
break its prison bonds and go on its way, rejoicing in
its wild freedom. Ask the little child, sporting among
the clover blossoms and singing birds, if it enjoys the
close walls of home as well as the green and flowery
fields. I, who love freedom so dearly, and love, oh! so
well, to muse over the lettered page, and forget the busy,
bustling world—how can I be content to teach school?
[*Growing excited*] To be imprisoned in a low, dingy,

dirty school-room, shut out from all that is beautiful and pleasant, and have to teach mischievous little witches how to read, write, and spell!

CLARA [*speaking surprised*].—Why, Lizzie, how you talk! I am perfectly surprised; calm yourself, do!

LIZZIE.—Well, you may be surprised, but it is so. I mean just what I say. What is there pleasant about it? Where, in the name of common sense, are the charms? And then the boarding around [*contemptuously*], I declare, it makes me sick!

CLARA [*smiling*].—A strong case, truly. Indeed! you are quite a lawyer. I am sorry to say, that I believe you are in earnest, by the way your eyes glow and burn. There is a dark side to every picture. You knew this before; why then did you teach?

LIZZIE.—Why, did you say? Why? Why does any one teach? To earn money, of course. If it were not for that, do you think I'd stay one week longer?

CLARA.—You have much to discourage you; so has every teacher. But, I hope, before long, the people will awake from their lethargy, and begin to act. Already a light has been kindled on the Hill of Science by a few, faithful, true, noble souls, and soon the beacon rays will light adown the hill, into the valley below. Then there will be more interest manifest; we will have pleasanter school-rooms, and more encouragement. I am sorry your main object in teaching is to earn money. Although we could not afford to teach without recompense, yet this should not be the main object; but oh! I fear it is with many.

LIZZIE [*scornfully*].—What then should it be?

CLARA.—Our reward consists not merely in dollars and cents, and not alone in an approving conscience, but in the pleasant smile, and the lighting of little faces at our coming, if we have done our duty and made our school-room attractive.

LIZZIE.—How can I make my old, dingy school-room

attractive? I guess it would need considerable remodeling.

CLARA.—Not merely, my dear, in adorning it with flowers, evergreens, pictures and mottoes to gratify please, and instruct the children; but in your kind smile, and heartfelt sympathy, and interest in their studies, sports, joys, and sorrows. Oh! Lizzie, the mission of the teacher is a great and holy one, and woe to those who attempt it thoughtlessly. Their prayer ought daily to rise to him who is ready to help for strength to rightly perform their numerous duties. They have immortal minds to sway. The influence and example of a teacher are remembered for ages, aye, through all eternity.

LIZZIE.—Thank you, for your words, Clara. I have never thought of the subject in that light before.

CLARA —Oh! Lizzie, may you often think of it carefully, soberly, and may success crown all your rightly directed efforts! But come, let us go to Mrs. Addison's. Supper and Lucy will be waiting for us [*smiling*]; and you dislike school-room and confinement so, I ought not to have kept you here so long.

[*They go out together.*]

MEMORY AND HOPE.

SCENE.—*A Poet—a boy in plain clothing seated at a table, leaning his head on his hands—pen, ink and paper before him.*

POET.—Write, write, write; I *must* write a poem, for thoughts come thick and fast. But why should I write? Memory is a haunting ghost I would fain have laid for ever. Hope is a delusive phantom I have parted with for the last time. "Hope and Memory, ye were once fair, but are nothing to me now!" [*His head sinks lower, and he seems to sleep.*]

[*Enter Hope and Memory. "Hope in a white dress with a wreath of white buds in her hair, and a bouquet of half blown flowers in her hand. Memory in dress of gray or drab barege, with a scarf of dark blue material thrown over her head, half shadowing her face; in her hand a bouquet of full blown roses and withering leaves. Memory turning to Hope, says:*]

MEMORY.—Oh, my sister, look at him wrapt in deep thought or gentle slumber! He feels my influence and knows it not. [*She waves her flowers over him, exclaiming:*]

"Float, sweet odors, about his brow,
And beautiful be his visions now."

[*Hope makes a gesture for Memory to stand aside approaches the Poet, and waves her flowers over him and says:*]

"Awaken, brother, and fix your gaze
Where flowers unclose when sunshine plays."

POET [*starting up*].—Who are ye that come into my presence thus, with your sweet picture-like faces, and voices like those I have heard in dreams? Speak and tell me!

MEMORY.—One who loves you—who watches by your pillow through the still night-watches, who is with you in that shadowy border land between sleeping and waking, whose hand points ever away, away to the sweet evening times of long ago; one who leads you away from the present along the fair, bright tracks where all is lovely.

HOPE [*drawing nearer*].—One whose smile beams upon you unceasingly, whose hand beckons you on where a sweet May-like atmosphere enspheres gardens of loveliness. There flowers fade not—there no dark clouds hover—there the spirit floats upward with the song of the lark—there even the midnight is glorious with stars. You have no friend like me?

POET.—Begone begone! you smile to deceive me

oh, Hope! You show me the past, oh, Memory, only to make my present more bitter! Away, I have done with you both!

HOPE.—Oh, hear me! To-morrow——

POET.—Tell me not of to-morrow. To-morrow never comes!

HOPE.—But to-morrow is always just before you.

MEMORY.—And yesterday ever near. Oh, the many many beautiful yesterdays I have to show you, lovelier now than when they passed away.

POET.—They passed away—Oh, sorrowful echo,—they passed away!

MEMORY.—But thou hast kept their smiles, their bright beaming smiles, and all the fresh lips and cheeks with their glow unfaded, and such sunshiny hair, and eyes with their love-light more tender than of old. Thou wouldst not lose all these?

POET.—I have lost all these.

MEMORY.—Nay, not so; they are now more near thee. Time and space can no longer divide; they come in a moment.

POET.—Their shadows come.

MEMORY.—But how real! They were once thine. They are thine for ever. Flesh or spirit, the same. They are still thine.

POET.—I would I could forget!

HOPE.—Listen to me, look toward the future. How bright, oh! how bright!

POET.—I wish not to look there. Thou canst show me nothing now. I know thee too well.

HOPE.—Oh! think of the green fields, the fresh winds, the unfolding flowers, the springing grass—all things full of glad life. The songs of birds as they build their nests, the laughter of children as they play along sunny lanes and in green fields.

MEMORY.—There are fair forms and sweet faces, welcoming voices, and hands kindly extended for thee, sunshine to gild, showers to refresh, and over all a rainbow.

POET.—Hush, hush, hush! [*He sinks down in a chair, takes a pen, and writes.*]

HOPE [*turning to Memory*].—What can we do for

him? I have been his ever true friend. I showed him the same pictures long ago that thou showest him now. Thou knowest all thy yesterdays were once my to-morrows

MEMORY.—Aye, sweet sister, 'tis so; and this poet is our special care. What strange whim has seized him that he would discard us both?

HOPE.—It is with to-day he is dissatisfied. I showed him all while it lay in the future, and he chose it then, calling it fair—very fair.

MEMORY [*laughing*].—See, sister! see, he writes. Oh! I have such a curiosity to see a poem where neither thou nor I shall be inwoven.

HOPE.—Be quiet. He has walked abroad in this to-day, and has written of it now, doubtless.

[*Poet, with an earnest face, thinking himself alone, reads his poem.*]

THE LEADERS.

The maiden read the spring time's idyl through,
  Each day's fresh page a fairer picture showing,
Flower-clustered branches, and nest-building birds
  And clouds in the blue sky with rose light glowing;
The rivulets ripple over mossy stones,
  And what the winds told to the listening leaves
When the dew touched them, and when moonlight brought
  The sweetest dream of heaven earth e'er receives—
The violet's passionate, pure prayer of love
  Thrilled her heart's chords; its sinless worshipper,
The arbatus, fair as light, and bright as life,
  Its Eden memories told again to her.
Yet scarcely smiled she all the while,
  Her heart was yearning toward a far-off grave,
Where slept her soldier youth—bitter thought!
  These flowers he loved so may not deck his grave.

[*He pauses, clasps his hands, and sighs. Hope and Memory aside.*]

HOPE.—I am there, and my dear poet has forgotten it.

MEMORY.—And I. How blind he is! but he proceeds. Listen to the second verse; see if we are exiled from it. [*Poet proceeds.*]

The mother read the sweet-rhymed poem,
  How royally rich was every page she turned!
The rose was crimson with the hue of triumph,
  The stars above as freedom's watch-fires burned.

But summer winds were sighing, ever sighing;
  And bead-like dew-drops rosaries were of tears,
For Tennessee's soft winds and low-toned waters
  Blend dirge-like in the strain her spirit hears.
There, far away, he sleeps, her gallant darling,
  Her hope, her pride, her bravest and her best—
Her blue-eyed first-born hushed to sleep so fondly,
  It seems but yesterday night, upon her breast.

HOPE.—We were both there!

MEMORY.—Yes, hand in hand!

HOPE.—What would that mother's heart be without me? I show her country's future!

MEMORY.—And how could she spare me? I still give her back her darling as I can, either as a babe or as a hero, beautiful, oh, how beautiful!

HOPE.—I point upward toward him, too—lead her even into the glorified presence of the gentle, brave-hearted boy, who learned how sweet it was to die for one's country, ere his sun had journeyed half way to its noon. But listen! [*Poet reads on.*]

And one in manhood's prime read the proud anthem
  Of autumn, ah! the tale was fitly told!
Of the bright mission in the laden orchards
  When fruit and leaves of bronze and red and gold
Made pretty pictures under the fair heavens,
  That through the Indian summer atmosphere
Smiled on the earth so fond; the soul upreaches
  To meet the angels, for they seem so near;
And 'midst those angels one is crowned with laurel;—
  That soldier son in Gettysburg that fell,
And autumn winds sigh softly, "It is finished;"
  And that fair angel whispers, "It is well!"

[*He pauses.*]

MEMORY.—Ah! how much of that is of me!

HOPE.—How much is of me!

MEMORY.—My voice is in the autumn wind that whispers "It is finished!"

HOPE.—And mine is in the angel whisper "It is well."

MEMORY.—And yet he knows not that I am with him ever.

HOPE.—And dreams that he has bidden me farewell

Hope and Memory [*together*].—Listen! [*Poet proceeds.*]

> O'er the calm-worded eulogy of winter
>   The gray-haired grandsire bent with earnest eye;
> And one by one, like snow-flakes floating, floating,
>   Came thoughts of how to live and how to die.
> Oh, Life, of thee the thoughts were *real, earnest;*
>   Oh, Death, of thee the thoughts were calm and high;
> Life's end and aim the Truth, our God, our Country,
>   Death but the entrance to eternity.

Hope to Memory.—Oh, sister, there we softly blend together!

Memory to the Poet.—Oh, Poet, call us each again your friend!

Poet [*advancing and clasping a hand of each*].—Oh, yes, for ever, ever, and for ever, let your sweet smiles upon my pathway blend!

A CONTENTIOUS COMMUNITY.

Scene.—*A country school-house, in which all the voters of the district have assembled to discuss some interesting topic relating to school matters.*

School Director.—Will some of the gentlemen who have been pleased to call this meeting, be kind enough to state to us its object?

Fairplay.—Mr. Merrysoul, Brother Orthodox, and myself signed the notice calling this meeting, in behalf of our singing master, who is desirous of opening a school among us this winter; as the gentleman is present, perhaps he had better speak for himself.

Music Teacher.—I have been desired to teach a class in vocal music, in this neighborhood; and the school-house being the usual place of assembly, as well as the most convenient and central room, I applied to the director to obtain the use of the house, and was denied it. Knowing this to be contrary to the wishes of the community, a number of my young friends have united with me in requesting these gentlemen to call a meeting to ascertain the opinion of the majority upon the subject.

School Director.—In refusing the use of the house for this purpose, I not only acted in accordance with my own convictions of right, but followed the advice of several of our oldest citizens, who think with me, that the school-house should be used for school purposes only

Fairplay.—This school-house, Mr. Chairman, was built by the community here for the accommodation of the wants and necessities of the neighborhood. It has been our custom from time immemorial to hold not only day school, but Sunday school, singing school, and religious worship in the house; and I can see no reason why a few persons should now seek to deprive us of our long-established right.

School Director.—The long prevalence of a custom does not, in my opinion, prove it to be right. We have used the school-house long enough for such purposes; it is time now to build another house to hold meetings in, and take care of our school-house for the use of the children.

Orthodox.—That is just what we wanted to do last summer, when we presented a subscription paper to you, Mr. Chairman, and you refused to sign a cent.

School Director.—The house you proposed to build did not suit my taste. It was not expensive enough.

Merrysoul.—I believe Brother Orthodox, in his plan, was trying to cut his coat according to his cloth; he knew it would be impossible to raise money enough to build a cathedral, and so he proposed to put up a plain church.

Wideawake.—The church Brother Orthodox proposed building was a frame, I believe; perhaps that was one reason why our worthy director did not like it, as he is the owner of that extensive brick-yard over yonder. However, the church is not built yet, and we want to have singing school this winter; and I, for one, am in favor of having it in the school-house.

Orthodox.—If I understand our worthy director aright, he would like also to exclude us from using the house for religious worship?

SCHOOL DIRECTOR.—I am opposed even to having preaching in the school-house.

HARDSHELL.—I don't mind having preaching in the house provided the right kind of preachers are invited to preach there.

MERRYSOUL.—I am not a member of any church; but for my part, I can not see why one denomination should be allowed the use of the house and not another. We all helped to build it, and I can not see why it should not be free for every denomination, and for singing school, too, as long as the property is well cared for.

HARDSHELL.—Well, if it came to excluding all or excluding none, I would allow preachers whose doctrines I did not approve to use the house, rather than have our preachers shut out from it. But this thing of singing schools I don't like. I shall not vote for our schoolhouse being used for it; nor will I allow my children to attend if these youngsters succeed in getting it up.

MERRYSOUL.—Why, Brother Hardshell, you seem to forget that David says, "Make a joyful noise unto the Lord." David was very fond of singing, and recommends it highly to all Christians.

MUSIC TEACHER.—I can not conceive why Brother Hardshell is so opposed to young folks learning to sing It is, I am sure, a healthful exercise and a pleasant pastime. A good singing school has a favorable influence on the morals of a community.

HARDSHELL.—I never learned to sing notes, and my children shan't. It will only make them inattentive to their books at school; and while I am losing their time from work to allow them to go to school three months in the year, I can not afford to have them waste their time, and divert their mind from their other studies.

SCHOOL DIRECTOR.—I reckon Brother Hardshell thinks that it would make the boys and girls lazy, and might create a desire to waste their mornings and evenings. If I mistake not, his children have to toe the scratch pretty close.

HARDSHELL.—That's so, gentlemen; if anybody lives with me they have to go to work, and no mistake. If I give my boys six hours out of the best of every day to go to school, they must work the harder between times and on Saturdays to pay for it, or I wont get my share of work out of them afore they are twenty-one.

TIGHTFIST.—Mr. Chairman, this is a digression. We had better proceed to the business on hand. I am much opposed to having another singing school in the house this winter, because they use up the wood we have to supply for the day school.

MUSIC TEACHER.—I would say a word here, Mr. Chairman, if you please. If I remember rightly, our singing class furnished a cord of wood last winter, and only met three times before the weather set in so bad that we thought best to adjourn until the roads had settled a little. When we commenced the school again, our wood-pile had disappeared; but, as it was warm enough to do without a fire, the class made no complaint about the matter. If we have the use of the house this winter, we expect to furnish all the wood we burn.

TIGHTFIST.—Besides this, Mr. Chairman, our benches were all badly broken up last winter, and, as they have been replaced by new ones, I am opposed to admitting these singers into the house again.

MERRYSOUL.—I happen to know something about that, Mr. Chairman; for on several occasions I had to bring some nails and a hammer to repair the benches broken by the children during the day, before we could accommodate our class at singing school. The carpenter that Mr. Tightfist employed to fit up our school benches last year, did a very poor job, and the children soon found out its weakness.

MULEBRAIN.—I don't like these musical gatherings. They always keep up such a singing that I can't go to sleep of a night for them; and my wife says that they keep her and the baby awake, too.

OBSTINATE.—I am of Mr. Mulebrain's opinion; for I have been at his house more than once when they had singing over here; and, though they did not care to go to sleep as early when they had visitors, I don't think these singers have any right to be disturbing the quiet of the neighborhood by singing schools, two or three times every week.

FAIRPLAY.—The truth of the matter seems to be this:

there are a few individuals in the neighborhood who are opposed to singing schools, and they wish to make all the rest of us knuckle down to them.

School Director.—The chief object of singing schools seems to be to gather the youngsters together for fun and social chit-chat.

Hardshell.—And to try their horses in going to and from the meetings.

Wideawake.—Perhaps Brother Hardshell forgets how natural it was for him to ride in a trot when he was young; but one would hardly think that as long as he limps along with that cane in his hand he would forget some of his later sprees.

Hardshell.—Now, friend Wideawake, you must not be too severe with an old man if he should be indiscreet enough to crack a whip as thoughtlessly while driving a pair of fractious colts as a yoke of sober oxen.

Orthodox.—We must not be too hard, my friends, on Brother Hardshell. We all know that there was a reason for that runaway scrape; and I hope that our brother will profit by the narrow escape he had and let "*Old Tanglelegs*" alone hereafter.

Hardshell.—Brother Orthodox touches a tender point there. I have always been used to having a drop at raisings and log rollings; and I don't think we could get along without it. Mereover, we have Paul's advice to take a little " for our stomach's sake and for our oft infirmities," and the Lord knows I have infirmities enough.

School Director.—Gentlemen, you are digressing again. Please return to the matter under consideration.

Tightfist.—I think, at least, the law should be taken to prevent these youngsters from riding along the road in groups and frightening and running over people's cattle. They almost ruined a heifer for me last summer.

Fairplay.—I think it would be well if the law would take hold of men who have hundred-acre farms, and yet make a barn-yard of the public highway; not only obstructing it, but endangering the lives of peaceable citizens who may be riding by on a gentle trot, while some silly calf takes it into its head to cross the road immediitely in front of the rider, as cows and calves invariably do when suddenly startled by the quick movement of a horse. If I mistake not, a steady, inoffensive lad almost broke his neck over the heifer referred to.

ORTHODOX.—Why, bless me, gentlemen, here we are off at a tangent again. Be calm, gentlemen. Don't let us get too warm. I think, perhaps, we had better decide the matter by a vote, without wasting more time about it.

SEVERAL VOICES.—Question!—Question!—Question!

SCHOOL DIRECTOR.—There is no motion before us, gentlemen.

FAIRPLAY.—Mr. Chairman, I move that we grant this gentleman the privilege of teaching singing school in the school house, provided the school furnishes its own firewood and takes care of the property.

MERRYSOUL.—I second that motion.

SCHOOL DIRECTOR.—Gentlemen, you have heard the motion. Those in favor of singing school being kept here, will please signify it by rising to their feet.

[*Twelve voters rise to their feet.*]

SCHOOL DIRECTOR.—Those of the contrary opinion, please rise.

[*Seven voters rise.*]

SCHOOL DIRECTOR.—The yeas have it.

HARDSHELL.—I thought it required a two-third vote to carry such questions.

SCHOOL DIRECTOR.—The majority rules.

TIGHTFIST.—I want to know who is to be responsible for the care of the house.

MUSIC TEACHER.—The one who has charge of the singing school will be responsible for the proper and careful use of the house and its furniture during the singing school.

TIGHTFIST.—The director must demand security Let him give security, and he can have the house.

FAIRPLAY and MERRYSOUL [*both together*].—I will go his security.

HARDSHELL.—I think, Mr. Chairman, that it is a great pity that old and respectable citizens like us, should be thus tramp'ed upon by these young upstarts. I intend to lay this matter before the School Commissioner, and I, for one, protest against your giving up the key for this purpose.

TIGHTFIST.—I also enter my protest, and more than this, Mr. Obstinate, Mr. Mulebrain, and myself, intend to form ourselves into a committee of three, to see tha this thing does not go on—peaceably, at any rate.

SEVERAL VOICES.—If the minority intended to rule why did you not tell us so before you put the thing to a vote?

WIDEAWAKE.—Come, come, gentlemen, this will never do. We will soon come to blows at this rate. If we can not have peaceable possession of the house, we will not have it at all. My best room is open to you, Mr. Music Teacher; and, indeed, my whole house, if it is needed. I shall take great pleasure in listening to and joining in your melodies.

SCHOOL DIRECTOR.—If there is no other business before the meeting, we may as well consider ourselves dismissed.

[*Exeunt Omnes.*]

LOST AND FOUND.

FATHER.—Here, Jennie, is a nice hood I found on Fifth Avenue; is it not one of the best sort?

JENNIE.—Certainly it is; but who could have lost it?

FATHER.—I suppose we will likely find an owner; but isn't it strange that any one would lose a hood?

JENNIE.—Was it not rolled up?

FATHER.—No.

JENNIE.—Well, father, you know it has been warm of late, and I suppose the lady has taken it off her head and been carrying it under her arm.

FATHER.—Well, Jennie, take care of it, and I think I will advertise it.

JENNIE.—Why, father, I should think the owner would do that.

FATHER.—Well, search the papers; perhaps it is already in. I must go to my shop.

[*Father goes off. Jennie gets a paper. Enter Miss Midwell.*]

JENNIE.—How do you do, Miss Midwell?

MISS MIDWELL.—Well, thank you. Are you reading the paper?

JENNIE.—Yes; I just took it up.

MISS MIDWELL.—Well, I will not hinder you. I just called to tell you Anna Wilkin wishes you to go and see her at her uncle's.

JENNIE.—Well! I hope I shall be able to do so. She is a noble looking lady, though I feel rather bashful in her presence, they are so rich.

MISS MIDWELL.—Oh, Jennie! don't think of the wealth of a person, when she is kind and sociable.

JENNIE.—Perhaps I should not; but I wish I had a nice hood to wear.

MISS MIDWELL—Oh! we were down at Hunter's store the other day, and they have such beautiful ones. Mother could not resist the temptation, and bought one for Lettie. You can suit yourself there, certainly; but good-by, I am talking so long.

[*Miss Midwell leaves, and father enters.*]

FATHER.—Any advertisement of that hood, yet?

JENNIE.—None that answers this one. I sent for the other papers; the same advertisement is in them all, but does not mention Fifth Avenue.

FATHER—I am very desirous the owner should have it.

JENNIE.—Yes. But since there is no owner appears, suppose I wear it. Anna Wilkin sent for me to visit her at her uncle's, and I can't think of wearing my old one there.

FATHER.—Put it on, Jennie, and let me see it. Is it a handsome one?

JENNIE.—Oh! very.

FATHER.—Is it not too handsome for you to wear? You know, Jennie, that I am not rich. You do not know that I am in debt, and it therefore would not be proper for you to wear an expensive article

JENNIE.—People will think it is a present.

FATHER.—Even that I should not like. We should dress according to our circumstances.

JENNIE.—A great many people, no richer than we are, wear very nice hoods.

FATHER.—I am very sure, Jennie, that no one whose good opinion is of any value, would think better of you for dressing expensively. This striving to imitate others is no mark of a dignified person.

JENNIE.—But what are we to do with it if I do not wear it? See, father! doesn't it look well? It fits me exactly.

FATHER.—Yes! it is very pretty; but I wish the owner had it. Are you sure it is suitable for you?

JENNIE.—Oh, father! it is exactly what I want. Some good fairy sent it to me, no doubt.

FATHER.—But I fear the Merchant's company that I expect to join, will not take me in if they see signs of extravagance on you.

JENNIE.—They nearly all know us, and I think will not be concerned about a hood.

FATHER.—Well, I will not object to your wearing it, if you are happy in doing so.

JENNIE.—Oh! thank you for your consent. I'll be off now to see Anna. [*Jennie goes off to Anna.*]

JENNIE.—Good evening, Anna.

ANNA.—Quite well. I'm glad to see you, Jennie. I trust we will have a good talk that will be profitable and interesting to us both.

JENNIE.—I hope so.

ANNA.—Are you acquainted with Fanny Bloom?

JENNIE.—Slightly. Is she not rather reserved?

ANNA.—She is a noble girl; at least I always thought her one of the most lovely girls that I know. It is a great pleasure to find a person acting out her own convictions, and living according to her means, without dressing in a certain way because her neighbors do, and never consulting circumstances at home.

JENNIE.—Yet, one does not like to be entirely different from other people. We judge of others by these outward things.

ANNA.—I confess that my pride would take that direction; but whe I see vulgar people striving to be fashionable, looking as if they carried all their possessions on their back, having no higher aim than to dress gay and expensive like their neighbors, I feel like dressing in serge and hair-cloth. My soul is sick of this mean ambition. How little they know of the true meaning of life!

JENNIE.—Y-e-s.

ANNA.—I am afraid you will think me rather severe, but I feel very deeply on this subject. I long to be a preacher of faith.

JENNIE.—"Of faith!"

ANNA.—Yes; of faith in something nobler and more satisfying than self and this outward world. Of faith in a Heavenly Father who gives to each his peculiar lot and duties. We are spoiling the beauty of his plan by striving too much to appear as other folks do. Pure and simple tastes are gratified at little expense, and a free and loving spirit gives itself forth to cheer, to comfort, and help others.

JENNIE.—Dear Anna, your soul-stirring words have reached my heart. Indeed, I feel all the time as though you were alluding to something about me.

ANNA.—I wish to give no offence by merely giving my opinion.

JENNIE.—Not at all. But this hood, I presume, you think is too costly for me; and I, too, am convinced that it is. Indeed, all the gems that are on it, only make me discontented. I shall not wear it any more.

ANNA.—But why not wear it since you have it?

JENNIE.—Father found it, and I insisted on wearing it. But the poor reproach me for doing so, the rich ridicule me, and my heart condemns me. If I could only find the owner how gladly I would restore it!

ANNA.—I have something to tell you, Jennie.

JENNIE.—What is it?

ANNA.—That is *my* hood

JENNIE.—Yours!

ANNA.—Yes. I knew it at once when you came.

JENNIE.—Oh, Anna! what an angel you are! How could you bear me in your presence? How you must have despised me!

ANNA.—I am glad to have you here, and hope I may never despise you.

JENNIE.—I wish I could be as good as you are.

ANNA.—You can; what can any of us do in this life but repent and strive, and look upward to One who knows all, and yet does not cast us off?

JENNIE.—I do repent, I do strive. I shall look upward as my only hope. A little more about the hood and I must go. I am so glad to find the owner, it will do me good to see you wear it.

ANNA.—No, Jennie, don't talk about me wearing it; I give it to you; you may do what you like with it. It has given you pain; perhaps in some way it may give you pleasure.

JENNIE.—How shall I reward you for all your kindness to me?

ANNA.—I am rewarded in the highest way; do not mention reward.

JENNIE.—If you insist on my accepting it, I think I will get it exchanged for something more "suitable," as father says.

ANNA.—Very well, just as you please. Your father will think well of you for doing so, no doubt.

JENNIE.—Certainly he will; and I must tell him soon what you have done for me. Good-by, dear Anna.

ANNA.—Good-by, Jennie; may we always love each other!

THE TRI-COLORS.

[Three little girls stand hand in hand under the canopy of the Star Spangled Banner, each with a small flag in her hand. The representative of RED, to be dressed in that color, with *roses* forming a wreath, and a bouquet: WHITE and BLUE, dressed appropriately, WHITE with *lilies* in bouquet, and white flowers in a wreath, and BLUE, with *violets.*]

RED, WHITE, AND BLUE [*speaking in concert*]:—We are three true-hearted, loving sisters. Our fame has spread over the earth, and foreign nations are proud to honor us. We float together, kissed by the rain sun and dew, from the mast head of the ships, that sail or the wide, blue sea; and we are ever welcomed and applauded, in every clime, and by every nation. As we near the port, many voices shout with joy and gladness, and the eye of the home-sick weary wanderer fills with tears of joy and welcome. Wherever seen, the heart of the patriot throbs with joy, for we bring thoughts and memories of that land where so many true men and women live, and where right and justice are calmly conquering wrong and oppression.

RED [*stepping forward*].—*I* am found in the glowing western sky, when the sun sinks to rest, and bathes the tree-tops and hills with glorious golden light. I bring visions of cheer and plenty as I linger among the orchards, and paint the mellow apple, and the luscious peach; and I enliven the landscape in autumn with my tints on the leaves in the forest. But I dwell in sweetest loveliness in the fragrant *rose*, which blushes amid the dark green foliage, and gladdens the heart of every lover of beauty; and on the fair cheek of youth and health.

WHITE.—*I* float in fairy forms in the pure clouds which rest against the vast, blue dome above us, and I hide my head with the modest *lily*. I am ever an emblem of innocence and purity; I enfold the beautiful form of the babe, whose innocent soul looks out from wondering eyes on our strange world, and I drape the limbs of the dead, who lie cold and still in their purity. I fall in snowy folds around the young bride, and whisper to her of love, and joy. My sister [*turning to Red*], I am with *you*, and we dwell *together* on the rounded cheek of youth.

BLUE.—Dear sisters, while the *lily* and *rose*, as your emblems, are blending in perfect loveliness on the fair cheek of youth, health, and beauty, I am sparkling in the ever-speaking eye, which tells its own language of sorrow and grief, joy and gladness. I am seen in the modest sweet-scented *violet*, which meekly bows its head to the world, and half hides its beauty from the careless gaze.

[*Again, in concert, with clasped hands, and in an exultant, joyful tone.*]

But we are *proudest*, and *happiest*, when all together we form the colors of *Our Country*. We dwell in the *dear old flag*, which now floats over a peaceful, *loving* people. Oh! the glorious flag,

"Long may it wave
O'er the land of the free, and the home of the brave."

[*The three unite in singing.*]

"Oh! Columbia, the gem of the ocean."

[The effect is the prettiest if the whole school each have a small flag concealed under their desks, and then join in the song, and at each chorus, "Three cheers for the red, white, and blue," wave their flags.]

ANNIE'S PARTY.

CHARACTERS.

UNCLE JOHN, ANNIE, FANNIE, NANNIE,
DORA, FLORA, FAITH.

SCENE.—*A bevy of little girls, hands joined in a ring Uncle John reading a paper.*

[*All—swinging in a circle and singing.*]

Ring round rosy in Uncle John's garden,
Uncle John is very sick, what shall we send him?

[*Uncle John covers his face with the paper as if asleep.*]

Three good wishes, three good kisses, and a slice of gingerbread
What shall we send it in?
In a golden saucer.
Whom shall we send it by?
By the Governor's daughter,
One that's down last tell whom she loves best.

ALL.—Oh, it's Fannie Day!

FANNIE.—I don't like this play; let's play something else.

ANNIE.—What *shall* we play? I never can think of any thing to play when I have a party.

DORA.—Button!

FLORA.—Dear me, that is so old!

ANNIE.—O, I'll ask Uncle John. He knows every thing. Uncle John—[*taking the paper from his face.*]—do tell us something to play, that's a darling!

FLORA, NANNIE.—O do, please!

FANNIE.—We can't think of any thing.

JOHN.—I'm very sick, Annie.

ANNIE.—O, that's too bad! I'll call mother.

JOHN.—No need of that. There were just now a rosy ring of fairies out in the garden, and they promised to send me some beautiful presents. I presume they will cure me.

NANNIE.—Dear! dear! Isn't he the funniest man you ever saw?

JOHN.—Perhaps you don't believe it! Such beautiful fairies—with blue ribbons, and green ribbons, and red ribbons, and pink ribbons—all turning round and round. You will soon see the Governor's daughter come in with my presents. I'm very fond of gingerbread.

[*All laugh.*]

DORA.—I shall die laughing!

JOHN.—Miss Dora, *will* you look out of the window and see if she's coming.

[*A knock at the door. Enter a fairy with a tray.*]

FAIRY.—[*Curtesying very low.*]—The flower-fairies of your garden, hearing of your illness, have sent you this little token of their sympathy; and in return for your kindness in giving water to the drooping flowers when they were fainting for cooling showers, they desir to grant you three good wishes.

JOHN.—It is very good of the flower-fairies to be so grateful, I am sure, and if I had known I was doing a kindness to such a beautiful young lady as yourself—

ANNIE.—Fie, Uncle John!

JOHN.—Excuse me, young ladies, I did not intend to slight you, for I am sure you are as charming as fairies, and to prove my regard for you, will you tell me what to wish for?

ANNIE.—Wish for as much gold as can be piled in this room.

JOHN.—That's modest, I'm sure.

NANNIE.—Wish to be President of the United States

JOHN.—Too much honor.

FANNIE.—Wish to be the wisest man in the world.

DORA.—Wish to be the happiest man in the world.

FLORA.—Wish for all the candy and nuts and raisins we can all eat.

[*They all laugh.*]

JOHN.—That's nice for me. But here's a little one that has not spoken a word this evening. What do you think is the best wish in the world?

FAITH.—Mother says we must always pray to be contented with what we have, and then we shall be happy. You better wish to be good and contented.

JOHN.—Little Faith is right. Miss Fairy, you can report to Queen Mab, that I wish to be very good and very happy; there are two wishes. I will take a basket of apples and candy for the third. [*Exit Fairy.*]

ANNIE.—What a beautiful fairy!

FLORA.—I do hope she will send us the apples and candy.

ANNIE.—But you must be very good, you know, Uncle John; so now tell us what we can play.

JOHN.—How would you like to speak pieces?

DORA.—Wouldn't that be splendid!

FANNIE.—What can we speak?

NANNIE.—Any thing we know.

FAITH.—Will Uncle John speak a piece too?

ANNIE.—Of course.

DORA.—We shan't excuse him.

JOHN.—I'm very sick.

FLORA.—No, the gingerbread cured you. You can't play sick any more.

JOHN.—I will see how I feel by-and-by. Perhaps—

DORA.—O, isn't he the *goodest* uncle in the world?

FAITH.—Annie must begin.

[*They all sit down, and Annie comes to the front of the stage.*]

ANNIE.—

    Uncle John is very sick,
    And what shall we send him?

FLORA [*laughing*].—O not that!

ANNIE.—

  There was an old woman went up in a basket
    Seventy times as high as the moon;
  What to do there, I could not but ask it,
    For in her hand she carried a broom.
  "Old woman, old woman, old woman," said I,
  "Whither, O whither, O whither so high?"
  "To sweep the cobwebs from the sky,
  And I'll be back again by-and-by."

DORA.—That was first rate. Now, Nannie.

NANNIE.—

    Dear sensibility, O la!
    I heard a little lamb cry baa,
    Says I, "So you have lost your ma!"
        "Baa!"

    The little lamb, as I said so,
    Frisking about the fields did go,
    And frisking, trod upon my toe.
        "O—oh!"

FANNIE.—

  Three little mice sat down to spin,
  Pussy passed by and she peeped in.
  "What are you at, my fine little men?"
  "Making coats for gentlemen."
  "Shall I come in and bite off your thread?"
  "No, no, Miss Pussy, you'll bite off our head."

DORA.—I can't think of any thing.

ANNIE.—Nonsense! I've heard you say lots of pretty verses.

DORA.—Shall I say "Children in the Wood?"
ALL.—O yes! That's splendid.
DORA.—

>My dears, do you know,
>That a long time ago,
>Two poor little children,
>Whose names I don't know,
>
>Were stolen away on a fine summer's day,
>And left in a wood, so I've heard people say.
>
>And when it was night how sad was their plight!
>The sun it went down, and the moon gave no light;
>They sobbed and they sighed, and they bitterly cried
>And the poor little things—they laid down and died.
>
>And when they were dead, the robins so red,
>Brought strawberry leaves and over them spread,
>And all the day long they sung them this song,
>"Poor babes in the wood! Poor babes in the wood!
>Ah! don't you remember the babes in the wood?"

ANNIE.—Now, Uncle John.
DORA.—Yes, you *must* speak now.
FLORA.—I shan't say one word till you do, and Faith won't.
FAITH.—No.
JOHN.—Then I suppose I must.

[*Coming forward with a bashful air, and making a stiff school-boy's bow.*]

>You'd scarce expect one of my age
>To speak in public on the stage;
>And if I chance to fall below
>Demosthenes or Cicero,
>Don't pick me up, but let me go.

[*Bows again and retires. All laugh.*]

ANNIE.—Now, Flora.
FLORA.—

>What does little birdie say
>In her nest at peep of day?
>"Let me fly," says little birdie,
>"Mother, let me fly away."

Birdie, rest a little longer,
Till the little wings grow stronger,
So she rests a little longer,
  Then she flies, she flies away.

What does little baby say
In her nest at peep of day?
Baby says, like little birdie,
  Mother, let me fly away.
Baby, sleep a little longer,
Till the little limbs are stronger.
If she sleeps a little longer,
  Baby too, shall fly away.

FAITH.—

I want to be an angel,
  And with the angels stand,
A crown upon my forehead,
  A harp within my hand.
There, right before my Saviour
  So glorious and so bright,
I'd make the sweetest music,
  And praise him day and night.

[*All the girls come to the front of the stage with their right arms round each other's waists, and sing the preceding stanza, and this:*]

I know I'm weak and sinful,
  But Jesus will forgive;
For many little children
  Have gone to heaven to live;
Dear Saviour, when I languish
  And lay me down to die,
Oh send a shining angel
  To bear me to the sky.

UNCLE JOHN.—The apples and candy are waiting in the next room.

[*Exit all.*]

THE RECLAIMED BROTHER; OR, THE CHAIN OF ROSES.

CHARACTERS.

HENRY BARTON. JAMES SMITH. ELLEN BARTON.

SCENE 1.—*A country store-room. Henry Barton and James Smith discovered.*

HENRY.—I'm glad you dropped in this evening, Jim. All the customers are gone now and we can have a nice little talk, all by ourselves.

JAMES.—I notice you have been kept very busy, and I suppose you are very tired by this time; therefore I'll not stay long. Are you going down to singing school to-morrow evening?

HENRY.—I'm afraid I can't get away. Mr. Hagan is in the city, and it is probable he will not be home until late to-morrow night. If he should get home early in the evening I can go.

JAMES.—I suppose you intend to take Lizzie Hall if you go?

HENRY.—Don't know yet—I guess I can't—if you have any notion of going that way to the singing, go ahead; I'll not be in your way. But, Jim, what do you say, will you have a drink of brandy?

JAMES.—Brandy? No, indeed! I never drink liquor of any kind. I hope you hav'n't taken to drink.

HENRY.—Oh, no, not at all; but I take a little sometimes for the good of my health.

JAMES.—Oh! is it possible? Henry you are treading on dangerous ground. Beware!

HENRY.—Pooh, don't be alarmed! I can take it or I can let it alone. Come, take a little drop, James: I have a bottle of first-rate stuff behind the counter.

JAMES.—Well, you may keep it there! Don't bring it out on my account, for I assure you I'll not touch it.

HENRY.—Well, you needn't get crankey about it; I wont insist on you.

JAMES.—I tell you again, Henry, you are treading on dangerous ground. You think there is no danger, but I know there is. I once heard a lecturer say that when a young man commenced to drink he wove a chain of roses around him which, in time, became a chain of iron that could not be broken.

HENRY.—Bah! Such talk always disgusts me. Do you think I hav'n't a mind of my own, and am able to drink or let it alone as I please?

JAMES.—I acknowledge that you may be able *now* to drink or let it alone as you please: but tell me, isn't it a great deal *easier* to take it than to let it alone?

HENRY.—Well—yes—no, I can't say that it is.

JAMES.—It may be as easy *now* to let it alone as it is to take it, but if you keep on drinking the time will come when you *can not* let it alone. You will come to like it more and more, and the chain will be drawn tighter and tighter around you, and it will be impossible for you to break it.

HENRY.—Do hush, James; I don't want to hear any sermons this evening.

JAMES.—I have commenced, and I want to say a few words more. You and I have always been good friends, Henry, and I hope we will be so still. Let me, therefore, advise you to take warning now. If you go on in your course you will break your sister's heart and bring down your aged mother in sorrow to the grave. They do not know that you are in danger. They look upon you with pride; but, tell me, what would they do and what would they say if they knew you had a bottle concealed in the store?

HENRY.—Well, to tell the truth, I suppose they wouldn't like it very much. I reckon they would get up a little scene; but then they are always troubling themselves about things that don't concern them. I think I am old enough to take care of myself.

JAMES.—Well, I suppose it is useless for me to talk to you any further on the subject. I see you are determined to take your own course. I will leave you; think over what I have said—think of the chain of roses which surrounds you now and think of the chain of iron which will soon surround you. Good-night.

HENRY.—Hold on, Jim—don't be in a hurry. Stop and take a pull of brandy.

JAMES.—I say again, *beware!* Good-night.

HENRY.—Good-night. [*Exit James.*]

HENRY.—Well, he's a puritanical sort of a fellow. He thinks I'm in great danger, but I know I am not. There's no use in a person being frightened before he is hurt. Well, I'll shut up shop and be off to bed.

[*Curtain falls.*]

SCENE 2.—*A room. Ellen and Henry Barton discovered.*

ELLEN [*weeping*].—Henry you came home last night intoxicated. How long must it go on thus? You promised me faithfully after our mother died, and after you were discharged from Mr. Hagan's employ, that you would never taste intoxicating liquor again. Have you kept your promise? Ah, if you knew how I feel when you come home intoxicated, I know you would never drink again.

HENRY.—Don't lecture me to-day, Ellen, I feel badly enough and there's no use in giving me any further trouble. I know I have done wrong, but it seems I can't keep from falling when temptation is thrown in my way. But don't talk to me; Ellen, my head is aching fearfully and I want to be quiet.

ELLEN.—I *must* talk, Henry. I beseech you, if you have any love for me, if you have any regard for the memory of our patient and loving mother, who is now in Heaven and who knows your every action, that you determine in your heart that you will nevermore touch the intoxicating bowl, and that you will strive faithfully to keep your promise, and then ask God to deliver you when tempted and he will do it. Oh, do not—do not, I beseech you, go on in the course you have marked out. It will bring ruin on yourself—ruin of both body and soul; whilst I, who have always looked upon you with pride will be led to despise you.

HENRY.—What's the use of making vows and promises when they are made only to be broken? I know I am doing wrong but I can't help it.

ELLEN.—But you *can* help it if you are only determined and if you strive mightily and ask God to help you. If you do so you *can* overcome and resist all temptations, no matter how strong they may be.

HENRY.—I used to think I could but I don't think so now. If any person had told me yesterday that I would be drunk before another day had gone round I would have considered him a fool. I had not tasted liquor for three months and I felt strong again. I believed I had entirely broken away from the band of iron that held me, and I felt and moved as a new man and as one who rejoiced in his strength. But in an unlucky moment I fell. As I was passing the tavern yesterday evening I met my old friend Jack Martin. He asked me to drink. At first I refused, but he insisted—"for friendship's sake," he said, and it seemed I *couldn't* resist. After I had taken the first glass it was very easy to take another and another, and I didn't stop until I was beastly drunk and had to be brought home by some of my friends. Oh, I heartily wish there was no liquor in the world, or that I had the power to keep it from my lips!

ELLEN.—Give me your promise once more, Henry, that you will strive to resist the demon intemperance, and that you will put your trust in God and ask him to help you. I know it is very hard to break away when the habit has once been formed, but it is worth while to try when there is so much at stake. Give me your promise again and I will pray for you—I will pray that you may always be able to resist temptation, and that you may live the life of a true and a good man.

HENRY.—Well, I give you my promise again, but it seems wrong to promise when my promises are so often broken. But I promise you that I will never touch the accursed bowl again.

ELLEN.—Strive to keep your promise, dear brother, and all will yet be well. [*Curtain falls.*]

SCENE 3.—*Same as second. James Smith and Ellen and Henry Barton discovered.*

HENRY.—Five years ago, James, you discovered that I was learning to drink. You had called in at Mr Hagan's store to see me and there discovered that the wine cup was luring me on to destruction. You warned me to leave off and not break my mother's heart. You told me that a chain of roses was being wound around me which would soon become a chain of iron. I heeded you not but went on in my downward career. A few months afterward I was discharged from Mr. Hagan's store, and a short time after that my sainted mother died sorrowing over her wayward son. I am employed again in Mr. Hagan's store and have regained the confidence of my employer. All I regret is that I did not take your advice that night in the store, and save my mother and sister the world of suffering they endured.

REFORMATION.

CHARACTERS.

POLICE OFFICER. SUPERINTENDENT OF REFORM SCHOOL.
TEACHER. JOHN WHITE, the boy.
JAMES CARR. JOHN WHITE, the man.   OLD NAB.

PART 1.

SCENE.—*Reform School—Superintendent in office, writing—James Carr sitting opposite, reading. Enter officer with boy, having long, uncombed hair, very dirty and ragged.*

OFFICER.—Good-morning, Mr. Superintendent! Here is another youngster to add to your numerous family.

[*Hands Superintendent the commitment, which he proceeds to read. In the meantime the culprit walks up to James Carr, and with a heavy blow with his fist knocks him off his chair. Both gentlemen pull him away rather roughly. Carr begins to cry lustily.*]

SUP. [*shaking him*].—What do you mean by such conduct as that, sir?

BOY.—I know'd that feller outside! He was put here for whipping his mother. He and I used to be "kinches" and went "snucks" on tappin' tills. One night he 'blowed" on me and I made up my mind to "lam" him the fust chance, and I've done it, only I want to get another lick at him!

Sup.—Well, sir, we don't allow such conduct here. And if you are guilty of it again, you will be severely punished. Step up here, now, and answer my questions. Mind you, tell me the truth, too, for I shall know in a moment when you tell me a lie. What is your name?

Boy.—"Yaller Jack!"

Sup.—That is not your right name, sir!

Boy.—Yes, 'tis; the boys all call me "Yaller Jack."

Sup.—I want your right name—the one your mother calls you.

Boy.—I hain't got no mother. The old woman calls me John White.

Sup.—What old woman?

Boy.—The one I lives with when I aint trampin' She says she's my aunt, but I guess she lies.

Sup.—What is this woman's name, and where does she live?

Boy.—They call her "Old Nab." She lives in Horse tail court, down by Water street.

Sup.—What does she do?

Boy.—Drinks rum, mostly. You see, I and Sal Lake board with her, and she sends Sal out every morning to beg and steal. She used to send me, too, but I've got so big now she can't come any of her games over me. I go on my own hook.

Sup.—Did you ever work?

Boy.—Yes, I set up ten-pins in Mike Dunn's alley for two months, but I got tired of that, and Mr. Smith's hostler gave me a job in the stable; but I stole his rum one night, got drunk, and sot the hay afire, so I got cleared out.

Sup.—Were you ever arrested before?

Boy.—Yes, a good many times.

Sup.—What for?

Boy.—Oh, for stealing and fighting. Old Jones got me "jugged," once, for setting fire to his barn, 'cause he horse-whipped me. I'll pay the old rascal yet.

Sup.—Did you ever attend school?

Boy.—I went half a day once, but the teacher didn't come.

SUP.—Do you know your letters?

BOY.—No; but I know how to play cards.

SUP.—Did you ever go to church or to Sabbath school?

BOY.—I was inside a church once, with Pat Mooney We got through the winder, and got a whole lot of books!

SUP.—How old were you when your father and mother died?

BOY.—Mother died when I was a little shaver. don't think I ever had any father!

SUP.—Come here, and let me examine your pockets. [*Overhauls his pockets and pulls out several plugs and papers of tobacco, a pipe, a pack of cards and a bottle of gin Sends Carr for teacher, who soon makes his appearance.*] Mr. Hayden, you will please take this boy and see that he is thoroughly washed and has his hair cut. Then burn those rags and have some clean clothing put on him.

[*Exit boy and teacher by one door; by opposite door enters an old, fat, red-faced Irish woman, half drunk. She goes directly to the officer and shakes her fist in his face.*]

OLD NAB.—Och, ye murtherin' spalpeen! What have ye done with me b'y? Sure and couldn't the little innocent go afther a little dhrop of ile for his old aunty's lamps without your stalin' him and bringin' him to thir horrible place. Bad luck to ye!

OFFICER.—You must talk to that gentleman [*pointing to Superintendent*]. The boy is in *his* charge now.

OLD NAB [*courtesying*].—I beg yer honor's pardon. out where is me b'y? I came to take him home wid we; and he has as beautiful a home as iver a b'y had in the wurrld.

SUP.—Why, madam, the officer says he caught him in the act of house-breaking. The boy himself says you taught him to beg and steal. This is the kind of oil you sent him after, [*holding up the bottle,*] and your face looks as if you had "struck oil," a little too often. I shall keep the boy, and if he behaves well, you will be permitted to visit him in the course of two weeks.

SCHOOLDAY DIALOGUES. 157

OLD NAB.—Och, ye two murtherin' villains I'll sa if I can't have me b'y, the little darlint that I have so tinderly brought up in the buzzum of the church! I'll sa Father Mahooney this blissed day, I will, and bad luck to yez.

[*Exit Nab and Officer. Enter John White, presenting quite a different appearance in his new suit.*]

JOHN [*admiring himself*].—Aha! I'm somebody now, aint I?

SUP.—You certainly *look* much better, and I hope you will try hereafter to *be* a better boy. To-morrow you will attend school, and work in the shop. Your privileges while here, and the length of time you remain here, will depend entirely upon your own conduct. You are not to be kept here for punishment, but for reformation. Your past offences will be overlooked. Here our rules forbid your swearing, fighting, or lying. For either of these offences you will be punished. On Sunday, you will attend church and Sabbath-school, and if you improve fast while here, you will in a few months be permitted to go out to a good home.

JOHN.—I'll try to behave.

SUP.—That is right. " I'll try" does wonders some times.

PART 2.

SCENE.—*Interval of twelve years. Schoolroom in same institution. Enter Superintendent, accompanied by a young man whom he introduces to the teacher.*

SUP.—Boys, I take pleasure in introducing to you Mr John White, who was formerly an inmate of this institution, but who is now engaged in study for the ministry You will please listen attentively while he entertains you with a few remarks.

JOHN.—My young friends :—Twelve years ago I came to this institution a poor, worthless outcast. Having lost my parents when quite young, I was thrown friendless and homeless upon the world. I was picked up in the street by an old drunken woman, who took me to her miserable hut and taught me to beg and steal that I might contribute to her support. I soon became an apt pupil. I found the transition from one crime to another gradual and easy. Stealing, swearing, and Sabbath breaking were my principal accomplishments. I was finally arrested and brought here. That was the first step toward my salvation. Here, for the first time, was I decently clad Here I was taught to read and work. In the Sabbath school, of which you are members, I was first taught the way of life and that I had an immortal soul. Here I found true friends, and these friends I have gratefully remembered through all the subsequent years of my life. When I came, I determined to reform. I obeyed the rules and improved my time. In less than a year a place was found for me with a wealthy and benevolent gentlemen, and ever since his house has been my home. Boys, this is your golden opportunity; strive to improve it. Listen to the teachings here imparted to you. Resolve that the past shall be forgotten in the good deeds of the future. By so doing, you will become useful members of society, and qualified to take your parts in the great Battle of Life.

[*The boys all rush up to him as he concludes, to shake hands, and the curtain falls.*]

SEEING A GHOST.

CHARACTERS.

NELLIE. SUE. MARGARETTA.

SCENE.—*Nellie and Sue sitting together in the evening, employed on some kind of fancy work.*

SUE.—I don't believe, Nell, there ever was such a thing as a ghost, you may say what you please. I never shall be afraid of encountering one.

NELL.—I hope you never will, but I believe there must be something in ghosts, or else there never would have been so many stories about them; beside, my Uncle Tom slept in a haunted house once, and a ghost came into his room and stood over the bed My Uncle Tom always spoke the truth.

SUE.—I don't doubt but that he *thought* he saw one, but I do doubt that he did, for I believe it was a ghost only of his imagination.

NELL.—Well, my mother once saw one walking in the grave-yard, and surely you wont think that imagination.

SUE.—Well, I believe it was either imagination, or some one who attempted to frighten her.

NELL.—Well, I think you are obstinate enough, and that nothing will convince you except experience; which I hope you may never have.

SUE.—If I should see any thing which resembled a ghost, I should be sure it was some one trying to frighten me, and I would find out if they were possessed of ghostly properties.

NELL.—I hardly think you would be as brave as the young lady who went into a tomb for the purpose of trying her courage, if you *do* think you would not fear a ghostly appearance.

SUE.—Why, what happened to her?

NELL.—Well, she took up a skull and commenced examining it, when a sepulchral voice sounded near, and said, "That's mine!" So she dropped the skull and took up another, and began an examination, when a voice said, "That's mine!" Instead of displaying fear she called out in a firm voice, "You fool, you haven't got two skulls." She had recognized the voice as belonging to one person.

SUE.—Oh, dear! I never want to go into a tomb any way, or touch a skull; but I'll risk all the ghosts. I'm glad I am not as superstitious as you are.

NELL.—So am I; for I am frightened always when I am alone in the evening, for fear I shall see a ghost.

SUE.—How silly! Who put such ideas into your head in the first place?

NELL.—My Uncle Tom is always telling ghost stories. When I was a a little bit of girl he used to take me on his knee and tell me most dreadful stories, till I cant help believing in ghosts.

SUE.—I am really sorry for you, Nell; but do try and banish such superstition.

NELL.—I *have* tried a great many times, but it does

no good. The other night I was obliged to walk alone a short distance in the dark, and on seeing something white, I was so frightened that I could scarcely walk, and I felt as if I should soon faint, when brother Will overtook me, and said my would-be ghost was only a white calf.

Sue.—I believe all ghosts, if seen in the daytime would be as far from any thing unnatural as that poor calf.

Nell.—I have often thought what I would say should I see such an apparition; but I presume it would all flee from me when the ghost appeared.

Sue.—I presume so. But what do you think you would do?

Nell.—I think I would talk to the white object in a coaxing manner, for I have heard they will leave much sooner than if one speaks harshly to them.

Sue.—Indeed! So you would use gentle means to rid yourself of their presence? I would do no such thing, I assure you.

Nell.—What would you do, then; command them? I have heard that they will be sure to haunt one who uses them unkindly.

Sue.—You hear great things, and such as I do not believe. But I wouldn't command them, I would only run to them and divest them of their white drapery, so that I might see who wished to play a trick on me.

Nell.—What if you should see it vanish away before you could touch it! Then would you believe in ghosts?

Sue.—Certainly.

Nell.—Oh, Sue! the clock has just struck nine, and I told mother I would be home at half past eight; but, really, it is so dark, and I am alone that I feel afraid.

Sue.—I will go with you and protect you from all the ghosts, for you know I am not afraid.

Nell.—I am so glad. Let us go now, for mother will be so anxious. But, hark! what was that noise?

Sue.—I heard nothing but the wind. Don't be so timid.

Nell.—Listen! there, you certainly heard that What was it?

SUE.—Nothing I——Oh! look! look!
[*Door opens slowly and a person wrapped in a sheet walks slowly into the room.*]

NELL.—Sue! Sue! you're not afraid; make it go way. [*Sue crouches behind her chair.*]

SUE.—Coax it, Nell. Oh! I'm fainting.
[*The ghost approaches nearer.*]

NELL.—My dear, kind ghost, wont you please— Oh-h-h!

[*The ghost approaches still nearer to Sue and stands still.*]

GHOST.—Never deny my existence again.
[*Goes out slowly.*]

NELL.—It is gone, Sue; but oh! wasn't it dreadful?

SUE.—More terrible than I ever saw before. I shall believe in ghosts after this.

NELL.—Who could help it? How I shudder to think of it? I shall not go home to-night.

SUE.—You must go alone if you do.

NELL.—And that I'll never do. [*Enter Margarette.*]

NELL.—Oh, Margarette! we were so terrified a moment ago. Sue nearly fainted, and I felt my senses leaving me.

MARGARETTE.—Why, what was the matter?

SUE.—We saw a ghost.

MARGARETTE.—Oh! don't talk so foolishly. There are no ghosts in this house, I assure you. You are very imaginative, to-night.

NELL.—No; we certainly saw one. I should think you might believe what both of us say.

SUE.—It came so near me that I could have touched it, and it was a ghost.

MARGARETTE.—Girls, I did think you possessed of a little courage; what you thought a ghost was only myself with a sheet wrapped about me.

NELL.—No, no; it must have been a ghost.

MARGARETTE.—If you can not believe me, I will play ghost again.

SUE.—Don't, I beg of you. It must be; but how foolish I acted. Why did I not run after you as I said I should and find out it was you?

NELL.—Well, if people can imitate ghosts as well as that, I shall think that there are not quite so many after all.

MARGARETTE.—I hope you will think so, and not be so timid after this. I think this will teach Sue not to boast of her courage again.

SUE.—Indeed it will. Come, Margarette, let us both go home with Nell. [*All go out.*]

THE MOTTO; OR, EXAMPLE.

SCENE 1.—*Two little girls seated at a work-table, one sewing, the other arranging a box of zephyr worsteds and silks. The name of the eldest* MARY, *the youngest* FANNIE.

FANNIE.—Sister Mary, our teacher told us yesterday that it was very unchristian-like to speak evil of the absent. Do you think it is?

MARY.—Yes, Fannie, I think it very wrong; and you know mamma never speaks evil of any one.

FANNIE.—Well, then, I think that lady who called to see mamma this morning is not a Christian, for she said so much evil about the governess of her children. Do you think she is?

MARY.—Indeed I don't know whether she is a Christian or not; but I know my sister Fannie is speaking evil of *her*, and the Bible forbids evil speaking of anybody.

MOTHER [*who had entered the room unperceived, and heard part of the conversation*].—Do you know in what part of the Bible it *is* forbidden, Mary?

MARY.—Yes, mamma, here it is [*turning over the leaves of a small pocket-testament, and reads aloud*]: James, fourth chapter and eleventh verse—" Speak not evil one of another."

MOTHER.—Well, Fannie, you wished me to find you a text for your marker; now I will give you this one to work.

FANNIE.—But, mamma, do *you* think it is so very, very wrong to speak evil ? [*Looking v inquiringly in her mother's face.*]

MOTHER.—I do, indeed, my daughter, think it exceedingly sinful. It is a violation of the moral law of God.

FANNIE.—But, mamma, when Mrs. Flipp was here this morning, and spoke so much evil about her governess you did—[*stopping, she looks down, and blushes*].

MOTHER.—You do not mean to say, Fannie, that your mother joined in the slander?

FANNIE.—Oh, no! No, mamma! You did not speak one word of evil, but——[*and again she looks down, colors, and is silent*].

MOTHER.—But, *what?* Don't be afraid, my love, but speak out candidly.

FANNIE.—Well, mamma [*looking up timidly*], you did not *look* displeased, and you smiled two or three times.

MOTHER.—Did I, my love? Then I did very wrong I will try to be more careful for the future, and endeavor to show by my manner and words, as well as by silence, that I think evil-speaking is a *crime*—and, as such, should be discouraged by all Christian people.

MARY.—Mamma, would it not be a good idea to have an Anti-Evil-Speaking Society?

MOTHER [*smiling*].—I think it would, my dear; and suppose we begin one in a small private way. We three will form a little band, and do all we can to overcome this fault in ourselves and others. What do you say?

MARY.—Excellent!

FANNIE [*exclaims at the same moment*].—Delightful!

MARY.—And, mamma, we'll appoint you President [*laughing*].

MOTHER.—Well, Mary, I accept the office, and appoint you Treasurer.

MARY.—Treasurer, mamma! Why, will there be any money to keep?

MOTHER.—There may be, although I hope there will not.

MARY.—I don't understand you, mamma.

MOTHER.—Well then, Mary, as I am President, I am going to make it a penalty of five cents fine for every time we speak evil.

FANNIE.—I know, mamma, you will never have any fines to pay.

MOTHER.—I am not quite so sure of that, Fannie; but I think this will act as a check, and make us more watchful. We will each have a small box, and the contents will be given to the poor.

FANNIE.—And may I give mine to poor old Sally mamma?

MOTHER.—Certainly, my dear, if you wish it; and I want you to remember, Fannie, if you ever take her gifts which your transgression of the law of love has earned for her, that I have known her for twenty years, and have never heard her speak one unkind word of any, although she has suffered a great deal from the unkindness of others. [*Then, turning to her eldest daughter, she said:*] Do you know, Mary, I have often thought that this poor woman would be a noble example for some who can boast of education and high position. And now, my daughters, as we are formed into a society, its name, as Mary suggested, shall be "The Anti-Evil-Speaking Society;" and its motto—what shall it be?

FANNIE.—Oh, please mamma, let it be the text you have given me to work.

MOTHER.—Yes, Fannie, we can not have a more suitable one—so our motto shall be: "SPEAK NOT EVIL ONE OF ANOTHER."

[*At this moment the parlor-door opened, and two morning visitors were announced—Mrs. Dash and Miss Brilliant. A few common-place remarks ensue, which the teacher of the dialogue can easily supply.*]

MRS. DASH.—I presume, Mrs. Belmont [*the mother of the little girls*], you have heard the all-absorbing "sensation" which is going the rounds—the elopement of Colonel Fast's son with his chamber-maid?

MRS. BELMONT.—No, I have not.

MRS. DASH.—No! Well, you are "late!" But it is a treat to come, for it is ridiculous in the extreme, and I am quite sure Miss Brilliant will relate the story in her inimitable style of portraying the ludicrous. Will you not, my dear?

Mrs. Belmont.—If Miss Brilliant will *first* do me a favor, I shall be greatly obliged.

Miss Brilliant.—Certainly, Mrs. Belmont; you have but to make the request.

Mrs. Belmont.—Thank you, dear Miss Brilliant, my daughters have to go to their studies, and Mary has expressed a great desire to hear you sing the exquisite anthem, which so charmed us all at Mrs. Cardini's, on Thursday evening last. [*Saying which she rose and opened the piano.*]

Miss Brilliant.—It will give me the greatest pleasure to oblige Miss Mary, who I hear is a very talented musician *in embryo*. [*Smiling, she seats herself gracefully at the instrument, and sings with great feeling, the anthem "I know that my Redeemer liveth."*]

Mrs. Dash [*who rises and glances at her watch before the last note has scarcely died away*].—I fear we will be late for our appointment at *one*, as I see it wants but twenty-five minutes of the time; so do, my dear Miss Brilliant, give us the story as quickly as possible?

Miss Brilliant.—Oh, not *now!* Mrs. Dash, [*imploringly,*] indeed I can not tell it at present.

[*Overcome with her emotions she bursts into tears. Little Fannie throws her arms around her and whispers in childlike simplicity;*]

Fannie.—Don't cry, Miss Brilliant, please don't cry any more. [*Miss Brilliant returns her caress and wipes her eyes.*]

Mrs. Dash.—Oh! I beg pardon most sincerely, Miss Brilliant; I did not know you had changed your mind, and I hope, Mrs. Belmont, you will excuse my being the innocent cause of getting up "a scene;" it is what I always studiously aim to avoid—no one can dread excitements more than I do—pray, excuse it, Mrs. Belmont.

Mrs. Belmont.—You have done nothing, Mrs. Dash, for me to excuse; and as to Miss Brilliant's feelings, those sublime words affected her too deeply to recite a frivolous, slandering story so soon after; she has endeared herself to my heart and gained my esteem.

[*The ladies now proceed to the hall, and as Mrs*

Dash advances, Miss Brilliant returns and whispers to Mrs. Belmont.]

MISS BRILLIANT.—Can I see you *alone* in an hour, if I call?

MRS. BELMONT.—Certainly, my love—come.

SCENE 2.—*Mrs. Belmont is seated alone in her parlor Miss Brilliant enters.*

MISS BRILLIANT.—My dear Mrs. Belmont, I was anxious to see you *alone* to explain my extraordinary conduct, you must have thought me very childish!

MRS. BELMONT.—Not at all, my love, I do not wonder at your feeling so deeply, such words, as you sung.

MISS BRILLIANT.—But I have sung them many times before, and was never so affected by them. In the first place, when I came here this morning, it was with a deep feeling of mortification. The last call Mrs. Dash and myself had made, she persuaded me to tell the ludicrous story of which they spoke to you. I did tell it, and as *she* would have said, in my "inimitable state," of course I had the plaudits of the fashionable gossips present, and felt elated; but just as we were about retiring, the ladies, thinking us out of hearing, their conversation turned upon myself. One lady made the remark—" Miss Brilliant is a most inimitable mimic." "Yes," replied another, "and I suppose *we* will be taken off, at her next call." "I was reading" said a third, "a few days ago, what an old author said about a talent for ridicule—'*If it is indulged in for amusement, it is foolish; if for revenge, it is wicked.*'" Mrs. Dash was busily engaged in conversation with the lady of the house, and did not hear the remarks; and I did not tell her, for I believe people seldom speak of that which mortifies their pride. When I was requested to tell you the same story, and you prevented it, I can truly say, I was deeply grateful, for I did not want to tell the story, but did not know how to get out of it. Now tell me, my dear Mrs. Belmont, had you not a design in asking me to sing the anthem? if you had, you took a most admirable plan!

MRS. BELMONT.—Yes; I had a design in it, I feel

myself religiously bound not only to abstain from evil speaking myself, but to discourage it in others whenever I can.

Miss Brilliant.—You will scarcely believe me, Mrs. Belmont, when I assure you, that although I have so freely indulged in this habit of ridicule and slander, I have always disapproved of it, and even when my praises have been the loudest. I have recently despised myself, for making merriment, like a buffoon, at the expense of others.

Mrs. Belmont.—I can very readily credit that those were your feelings, for you were acting out your lower nature, and neglecting to develop your higher capacities; and at the same time when we transgress any of the *moral* laws, there is a conscious feeling of degredation which humbles us in our own estimation, and this is a wise check from our Maker.

Miss Brilliant.—When I seated myself this morning at the piano, it was with such a keen feeling of mortification, and with such a sincere wish to renounce for ever this abominable practice, that I saw the beautiful words of the anthem in a light I never viewed them before, and I longed to have strength from heaven to resist the wrong, and do right for the future. And these emotions, when Mrs. Dash asked me to tell the story, were the cause of my strange behavior.

Mrs. Belmont.—I can not tell you, my dear young friend, how happy this statement has made me, for you, thus feeling your own weakness, and looking above for your strength, will obtain the " wisdom" spoken of in James, 3d chapter, and 17th verse.

Miss Brilliant.—And will you not, my dear Mrs Belmont, be my friend and counsellor, and help me to begin life anew?

Mrs. Belmont.—I am your sincere friend, and if I am capable of giving you counsel or aid at any time, I will most cheerfully do it; but your greatest help must come from on high, for the Maker of the human heart is surely the most powerful Regulator of its emotions, and " from the abundance of the heart, the mouth speaketh." [*Mrs Belmont then rose, and handing the marker partly worked by little Fanny, said*]: I and my children have formed ourselves into a bond, which we have playfully called the "Anti-evil Speaking Society," and the motto which Fannie is working on this marker is to be, "Speak not evil one of another." We are all pledged to do what we can to discourage evil speaking in ourselves or others, and every time we transgress, we will have to pay a fine of five cents. This will act as a check, and to remind us of our duty.

MISS BRILLIANT.—Oh, that is a most admirable idea! an Anti-evil Speaking Society—and original, I suppose.

MRS. BELMONT.—No, it originated with Mary; she suggested it, and I suggested the fines.

MISS BRILLIANT.—I wish you would let me join it, Mrs. Belmont, for I need all the checks I can have, to overcome my besetting sin.

MRS. BELMONT [*laughing*].—With all my heart, my dear. The children have made me President, so I'll enroll your name at once.

MISS BRILLIANT.—Well, Mrs. Belmont, it is the first time that I ever felt a wish that the poor should not be benefited. I really hope they wont get a cent from me, but I fear they will get dollars.

MRS. BELMONT.—If there is not one cent finds its way to the box as a *fine*, I propose, as the President, that we place dollars for the poor in another box, as a thank-offering for being delivered from so gross and degrading a crime! I can call it by no better name.

MISS BRILLIANT.—Our motto at a distance, may do very well for others, Mrs. Belmont, but as for me, I must have it very *near* me all the time; so I will just call on my way home [*rising*] and hand *this* to the jeweler, [*taking a heavy plain gold ring from her finger,*] and have these words engraved upon it—"*Speak not evil one of another.*"

CHOOSING A TRADE OR PROFESSION.

CHARACTERS.

HALL.   SWAIN.   DEAN.   MEEKS.   TEACHER.

HALL.—Say, Swain, who, that is now in this school, will make the greatest figure in the world? Do you think there is one that will ever be President of the United States?

SWAIN.—Your questions, Hall, are easier asked than answered. You know as well as I who are the best scholars, who are the best in the ball alley, and who are the most popular every where about the school.

HALL.—Do you believe there is one that will ever be a member of Congress, a governor of some State, or even a member of the Legislature?

SWAIN.—I do not know about that. Time often brings about wonderful things. Lincoln never attended as good a school as this; and perhaps I might say the same of Washington. But these great and good men made the best use of such opportunities as were in their reach. They were more studious than some in this school.

HALL.—Now, Swain, I know that you intend to be something in the world; what would you like best to be?

SWAIN.—I think that I shall be well satisfied with farming.

HALL.—What! with all the scientific learning that you will acquire in ——— [*here use the name of the school where this piece is spoken,*] and perhaps a college course besides, and A. M. attached to your name, would you then condescend to be nothing but a country clodhopper?

SWAIN.—Don't speak in such disrespectful terms of that business which is the main source of every body's living. Before you talk so, learn to live without eating or wearing any thing that has grown on a farm. Some of our best men have been farmers. Some of the best governors and members of Congress have been invited to those exalted positions from rural homes. When a man is thus honorably promoted from a secluded home, if he have the benefit of a good scientific and literary education acquired in his youth at some good institution, how great his advantage! And then no one leads a more honorable and independent life than the farmer. If he be a scholar, and take delight in scientific and literary pursuits, he can find entertainment with his books, while his crops are growing. Think of Washington, who, after gaining the independence of his country and aiding in establishing a new form of government, then retired from public life and engaged in agriculture.

HALL.—I see the force of your reasoning. [*Enter Dean.*]

DEAN.—What now, Swain? you seem to be giving a touch of the sublime!

SWAIN.—I was just setting forth some of my ideas about farming as a business.

HALL.—Yes, Dean, and he has almost persuaded me to be a farmer.

DEAN.—It would be well if many people who are looking to some profession that they imagine will be genteel and dignified could be altogether persuaded to be satisfied with life on a farm; even some now in this institution.

HALL.—Do you include me in that list?

DEAN.—I mean no personalities, but future time and circumstances will disclose what position you and others in this school are best adapted to fill.

HALL.—Now, since the subject is fairly opened, tell me, Dean, what business would you like best?

DEAN.—I'll tell you some time. [*Enter Meeks.*]

MEEKS.—Talking about business, are you? well, then, let me join your company, and hear some of your ideas about the pursuits of life.

SWAIN.—All right, Meeks, what have you in view?

MEEKS.—I am not yet fairly decided about that. I intend first to get a good education, and then see what prospect opens for me. What do you intend to do, Hall?

HALL.—I intend to graduate; then pitch into legal

studies, and after practicing law for a few years, I will aim for going to Congress.

Dean.—It will be well for you, if your means are equal to the wants of your ambition. You may very much miss your aim.

Hall.—You know the saying— ' He who aims at the sun may not reach his object, but he will be likely to shoot higher than if he aimed at something on the earth.' So if I never reach the Senate, I shall expect to attain some position higher than common life.

Dean.—You would do well to bear in mind the fact that some of our would-be-great men have used themselves up in just such ambitious schemes as you now entertain, and then did not attain the grand object of their wishes. If every man went to Congress that wishes to go, Washington City would not hold them all; but if none were allowed to go, but such as are well qualified, I believe that there would be many vacant places in the Capitol.

Meeks.—Hold on, or you may discourage him in his grand projects.

Dean.—Well, then, I will change the subject. I suppose that you look to the ministry.

Meeks.—I will not say that I do, nor that I do not I intend, after graduating, to proceed as Providence opens the way.

Swain.—That is sensible, Meeks. I hope the right thing for you will soon be opened to you.

Hall.—If he looks to the ministry, why not decide on it now, and then look to the pastorship of a good church, or perhaps a bishoprick?

Swain.—Time enough to think about that after a few years of successful pastorship in a common church, or a few years of circuit-riding. He might be very useful in either capacity.

Dean.—Well, it takes all kinds of people to fill the world. We must have farmers, mechanics, merchants, and professional men. All are useful in their places.

Hall.—The most of our students are looking to some of the learned professions. I suppose that I shall have the pleasure of calling you Doctor Dean sometime.

Dean.—Wait till you see that on my sign, and

the emblems of a physician's office in my windows [*Enter teacher.*]

TEACHER.—Young gentlemen, I have overheard a part of your conversation about the choice of business. A judicious choice in this particular will be one of the greatest things of your lives. If you wish for some of my ideas about it I will tell you what they are with pleasure.

MEEKS.—I would like to hear you.

ALL THE OTHERS.—Go on! Speak on!

TEACHER.—I believe that all persons are designed to be useful in some way; and every person in his pupilage should strive to ascertain what this particular vocation is likely to be. Your studies should develop your abilities and capacities, and your learning should qualify you for future usefulness, and for living in such a way that the world will be the better for what you shall have done in your lifetime. A man's life is a failure when after his death it can be only said of him that the world has not been benefited by his having lived in it. Consider now the character of the different pursuits of life, and what is necessary for success in each of them; and your ability and adaptation in them, as well as their respective uses; then may you expect to learn where and how you can be most appropriately employed. It is wise to trust in Providence. When your merits and your acquirements become well known, you may be invited to some dignified and honorable position in church or state that you do not now anticipate. To whatever you look do not despise labor. Farmers and mechanics are the bone and sinew of a nation. They should be educated as well as any others; they, too, can enjoy scientific and literary pursuits as well as any people. Do not despise labor because you have a scientific education. Do not foist yourselves into some of the learned professions because they appear to you genteel and dignified. Some of them are now too much crowded. The Christian ministry is truly a noble and glorious calling. It may not advance you to wealth, but by it you will do good for your fellow-beings, and have the blessing of heaven to rest upon you. Other professions and all trades look mainly to the acquisition of wealth; and I need not now speak of the demoralizing influence of inordinate ambition for this. But I will remind you that a rational education will counteract this and all other evil influences in the different vocations of life.

It is not for me to dictate what should be your chosen vocation, but your natural inclination, your acquired learning, and the judgment of your wise friends who will sometime see your merits, will direct you to the place that you should fill. Young gentlemen, I now leave the subject with you; think about it and act according the best of your judgment. [*Exit Teacher.*]

DEAN.—There, fellows, what think you now about choosing a trade or a profession?

SWAIN.—The more I think of agriculture as an employment, the more interest I feel in it. I endorse the language of my favorite poet:—

> "Oh, knew he but his happiness, of men
> The happiest he! who far from public rage,
> Deep in the vale, with a choice few retired,
> Drinks the pure pleasures of the Rural Life."

That's the life for me. [*Exit Swain.*]

MEEKS.—As for me, I hope to see my way to honor and usefulness when I finish my scientific studies But now I feel an inward monition that says, *Live not in vain!* Live to do good! But I can not now say much about it. [*Exit Meeks.*]

HALL.—Swain and Meeks seem to be quite set on leading a humble career; and how eagerly they swallowed the teacher's discourse!

DEAN.—They take quite a common sense view of trades and professions. What do you think now about your schemes?

HALL.—Not discouraged! A few years after I graduate at ——— [*here use the name of some college often talked about where this piece is spoken*] perhaps you will hear from me.

DEAN.—When you reach the pinnacle of your glory, remember those who were once your fellow-learners in this school, and then come and visit me in my humble abode. [*Exeunt.*]

CHILD-PHILOSOPHY.

Lillie.—I shan't stand it! I wont! I do declare! It is the most absurd thing I ever knew! If it is not enough to provoke a saint!!

Mina.—What is that, Lillie? Did you say you were going to be a saint?

Lillie.—No! any thing but that!

Mina.—Why! Did you not say you felt like a saint?

Lillie.—How should I know how saints feel? It is bad enough to feel like one's self, and I know that I feel very much provoked!

Mina.—Why, that is funny!

Lillie.—Well, I don't see any fun in it!

Mina.—But, see here, Lillie; tell me what——

Lillie.—Don't talk to me! I am too much vexed!

Mina.—But, Lillie, do tell me—what has annoyed you so much—come! What is it? You will tell me? Won't you!

Lillie.—Why! people treat me so!!

Mina.—Do they? That is too bad! What have they done?

Lillie.—Why, they think at our house that I am nothing but a little snip of a girl! They think they can say any thing to me! I am of no consequence at all! And here I am, nearly ten years old! And you see how very tall, and womanly looking I am! I think it is abominable!!

Mina.—Well, so it is, Lillie!

Lillie.—Oh, yes! I must be good! I must not be rude! I must do every thing, just so! and yet, when I want any thing—Oh! I am only a little girl!!

Mina.—It is too bad!

Lillie.—Don't you tell any body, Mina! There is my sister Bell—(now, if she is a young lady, why shouldn't I be?) She went off to Saratoga with trunks full of dresses and mantles and shawls, waterfalls, Grecian curls, nets, (oh, beauties!) two new bracelets, embroideries, handkerchiefs, and all kinds of bright ribbons, and every thing nice!—and I——

MINA.—But Bell is eight years older than you are, you know?

LILLIE.—That is nothing! Age has nothing to do with it! If it had, why doesn't mother go off and dress and ride and have good times? But here I am, expected to behave like a *lady*, and I ought to be treated like one!

MINA.—Well, is that all? Have you told me all your troubles?

LILLIE.—No! not half! There is my brother George, he talks to me as if I was good for nothing but waiting on other people. Just a little mite! Calling out Lillie, here! or, Lillie, there! Bring me this! or, bring me that! I don't mind running up and down stairs for him, and helping him, for he is real nice, and bringing him his slippers and his papers and his dressing-gown and his cigars and his cane and his books and his Florida water! But then, why doesn't he take me out riding with him in his new wagon? Why doesn't he ask me to walk in the park? Why don't I sit up late at night in the parlor? I think I deserve it—don't you?

MINA.—Why don't you speak to your brother and sister, and tell them how you feel?

LILLIE.—Yes! That is just what tries me so! George gives me a paper of candy, and says I look so small— that it sounds cunning to hear me talk! And Bell says, Pshaw! child! run away, and play with your dolls! You must not think about such things for years to come!

MINA.—What does your mother say?

LILLIE.—Oh! mother says I am only making trouble for myself—that these are my happiest days. But, dear me! how can that be?

MINA.—I guess she is right, Lillie! That is just what my mother says!

LILLIE.—Well, I don't believe it! If people mean what they say, why don't they act it? If they are happiest at home, why don't they stay at home? If fine clothes are such a care and trouble, why do they have them? If sitting up late at night injures their health, why don't they go to bed at eight o'clock, like me? If jellies, and creams, and pickles are so very good for older people, I don't see how they can be so very bad for me? Oh, I don't think a few years ought to make such a difference! And I tell you I am not going to stand it! It is not right! If I am nothing but a child, let me act as a child! And if I am a little woman, then treat me as a woman; and I shall never be satisfied until they do!

THE NOBLEST HERO.

DRAMATIS PERSONÆ.

MR. MANLY, the schoolmaster.
MRS. TRUMAN.
FRANK TRUMAN,
JOE MARTIN,
HENRY MORLEY,   } Scholars.
CLARK RICHMOND,
LEWIS HERMANN,

SCENE 1.—*School-room, class standing.*

MR. M.—Now, boys, I promised you a new study for Monday, and as it is Friday I will give you the subject now. It is—What Constitutes the True Hero—and you may, if you choose, give an example of the noblest hero of whom you have ever read.

FRANK.—May we ask our friends about it, or must we find out for ourselves?

MR. M.—I prefer that you should find out for yourselves.

HENRY.—We may look in books, may n't we?

MR. M.—Certainly. Any books which you can find to give you any light upon the subject. It is the hour for dismissal; put away your books, and when you come out be sure to lock the door. [*Exit Mr. M.*]

CLARK.—Who under the sun is the greatest hero? I can't guess.

LEWIS.—You're not expected to *guess*, you're to *think*.

JOE.—It is not very hard. I think I know mine already.

FRANK.—I should know mine if I thought Mr. Manly

SCHOOLDAY DIALOGUES. 177

meant what we are thinking of. But he smiled so oddly when he told us the subject, that I suspect he means more than we think he does.

CLARK.—Well, come home; we can talk it over afterward. I am as hungry as I can be. [*Exit all.*]

SCENE 2.—*A parlor simply furnished. Mrs. Truman and Frank Truman sitting at a table. Frank in deep thought.*

FRANK.—Mother!

MRS. T.—Well, Frank! what is it? You seem to be more thoughtful than usual.

FRANK.—Yes, mother; because our new teacher gave us such a queer subject for our lesson next Monday morning.

MRS. T.—Well, what was it, Frank?

FRANK.—It was—What Constitutes a True Hero— and I can not make up my mind; and we are not permitted to ask anybody.

MRS. T. [*smiling*].—Well, Frank, then I am afraid I can not help you.

FRANK [*leaning his head on his hand, thinks; but suddenly jumping up exclaims*].—I have it! I have it mother! [*Runs from the room.*]

MRS. T.—I am sure I hope he has, as he has tried so hard. [*Exit Mrs. T.*]

SCENE 3.—*Monday morning, the street before the schoolhouse. Enter Henry and Lewis at opposite doors.*

HENRY.—Well, Lewis, have you your hero?

LEWIS.—Yes, indeed, Henry. It did not take me long to think who I should have.

HENRY.—Well! where are the others? It seems to me they'll be late if they don't hurry.

[*Enter Frank, Clark, and Joe.*]

LEWIS.—Here they are! Good-morning!

JOE.—Got your hero, Lou?

LEWIS [*slapping his jacket*].—Yes, all right; safe here in my pocket.

CLARK.—He must be a precious small hero if he is in that pocket.

LEWIS.—He may turn out bigger than yours, who knows? though he is in such a small space.

FRANK.—Yes, Lou is right; it is not always the largest bundle which contains the most valuable article [*Enter Mr. M.*]

HENRY.—Well, here is Mr. Manly.

MR. M.—Good-morning, boys!

ALL.—Good-morning, sir.

MR. M.—I hope your heroes are all chosen?

ALL.—Yes, sir; we are all ready. [*Exeunt all.*]

SCENE 4.—*School-room. Boys seated.*

MR. M.—Well, boys, I'll call upon each in turn for his idea of what constitutes a hero, and for your chosen one. Well, Joe, you may speak first.

JOE.—I think, sir, that heroes should have great talents, and should never be afraid of any one; but should conquer all their enemies.

MR. M.—Well, certainly, you are quite right, as far as you go; but have you not omitted any thing?

JOE.—I could not think of any other necessary quality, sir.

MR. M.—Well! we will hear what the others say; but who is your hero?

JOE.—Alexander the Great.

MR. M.—Truly you have chosen a great conqueror; but I am afraid he lacks some qualities which I should wish my hero to have. Now, Clark, tell us your definition.

CLARK.—I think, sir, that a hero should be generous and forgiving; but, at the same time, firm and undaunted, and should love his country more than his life. And I have chosen Washington.

MR. M.—Very well, indeed, Clark, your definition is good, and your choice is a noble one. Now, let us hear Henry.

HENRY.—I, sir, have chosen Cromwell; but I fear he is not the right kind of hero, as I think he fought for himself quite as much for the liberty of the English from Charles the First's tyranny. Though I did not think of that before Clark spoke.

MR. M.—I believe you are right, Henry, though it is

a disputed point whether he did all for himself or not. Now, Lewis, who is your hero?

LEWIS.—I, sir, chose Washington, but as Clark has taken him, I will choose Abraham Lincoln, who was so kind and merciful, so just and good that he can stand side by side with Washington in our love and respect.

MR. M.—Very well, indeed, Lewis. I am much pleased that you should have chosen him. Now, Frank, tell us your thoughts, we have heard all the rest.

FRANK.—I, sir, thought for a long time over all the heroes of ancient times, but none suited me; they all wanted something. Then I thought of the Bible verse: 'He that is slow to anger is better than the mighty; and he that ruleth his spirit than he that taketh a city." I took that as my definition, and I add to it generosity, self-devotion, and self-sacrifice.

MR. M.—Truly, Frank, you are right. For [*turning to the audience,*]

"The noblest Hero of the whole
Is he who can himself control."

[*Exeunt omnes.*]

WOMEN'S RIGHTS.

CHARACTERS.

Five Boys.
POLLY SIMPSON, a tall, slender spinster.
NANCY LAWRENCE, a strong-minded lady.
GRANNY SNARL, a slender spinster, with a blue cotton handkerchief bound tightly around her head, and tied in a bow knot behind.
SIMON VILDERBLOWS, a small, inferior-looking old bachelor.
[All seated near a desk, excepting the boys, who are in the back part of the house.]

POLLY SIMPSON [*rising*].—The first thing in order will be to choose some one to preside over this meeting. I nominate Sister Snarl for president.

NANCY LAWRENCE.—I second the nomination.

POLLY SIMPSON —It is moved and seconded that Sister Snarl be president of this meeting. If this be yer minds, please manifest it by saying aye.

ALL.—Aye! aye!

POLLY SIMPSON.—'Tis a vote. Sister Snarl will now take the desk.

[*Granny now marches to the desk, while Polly takes a seat at her elbow.*]

GRANNY SNARL.—Sister Simpson will now read ye the resolutions.

POLLY SIMPSON [*rises and reads*].—*Resolved*, That the awful state our country is in, bids us wimmen folks do something right off.

Resolved, That as, under the present rule of the men, we are already in a deplorable condition, which grows worse and worse every day, we wimmen folks will take matters in hand, seize the reins of government, and make better steerage than they do.

Resolved, That to put a stop to this war, and to make peace, which shall be thorough and endurable, and to bring down vittals and things, so as not to have so many paupers for the town to support, we will go to the ballot-box at the next annual town-meeting, and elect, if possible, competent women to take charge of the public business.

GRANNY SNARL.—If it be yer minds to accept these, you'll please say aye.

ALL.—Aye! aye!

GRANNY SNARL.—It's a vote. Sister Simpson will now continue her remarks.

POLLY SIMPSON [*hemming and bowing, and clearing her throat, proceeds to speak*].—*Fellow-citizens:* This is an awful state that our country is in just now, and every thing is growing worse and worse. Goods, and such like, are so dreadful high that we'll soon be unable to live at all, and it's all owing to the mismanagement of the men folks. Now, if we wimmen folks take things in hand, and follow these resolutions, things will soon get to going straight along, and then decent folks can live. The men folks have *mismanaged* the business long enough, but the wimmen folks must *manage* it hereafter.

GRANNY SNARL.—Mrs Lawrence will now express her views of the subject.

NANCY LAWRENCE.—You all know that what Sister Simpson has said is true Our country is in a deplorable condition, just on account of the mismanagement of the men folks now-a-days. Why, when my first husband, Mr. Whitecomb, was alive, I was happy, and had the good times. Ah! I then had a kind companion; he knew how to manage an' keep all strings a-pullin'. But times, alas! have changed. I now have to look out, not only for number one, but for number two, also. I have to work like a dog, an' see to all the business myself 'cause if I didn't every thing'd go to rack and ruin. It's no use to arguefy the p'int—no use at all—something's got to be *done*, and that something right straight off, as Sister Simpson says. I've no more to say. Let deeds, not words, be our battle-cry.

GRANNY SNARL.—We will now hear what Mr. Vilderblows has to say on the subject.

SIMON VILDERBLOWS.—Things is going on to ruin as fast as they can go, fellow-citizens, an' I'm most dreadfully afeard it's owing, as has been told you, to the mismanagement of us men folks. I, for one, approve of letting the women rule. Do this, and my word for't, things will get cheaper, and poor folks like us'll have some chance to live. Yes, my friends, pork is gettin' to be monstrous high. Bimeby we shan't have enough to put into baked beans, and then what shall we do? I don't know what we shall do unless we put in *pitch-knots* instid of pork. Western pork, they say, is fattened on rattlesnakes, and who wants to eat serpents 'long o' their tea an' coffee? As to raising our own pork, why, corn, p'taters, an' sich like, is so awful dear and skerse, that if it so happens we do have a little to spare, we're obliged to take it to buy West Injee goods, and so forth. Then if we kill our hogs in the full of the moon, it'll shrink, you know, and there, again, is a loss. I raised a nice spring pig this year, and t'other day, as we's most out o' meat, and he'd got to be fat's a poirpoise, I thought best to kill him. So I put on the water a-heatin', got the scaldin' tub an' other things ready. Well, says I to John, my hired man, it's now full moon, an' some say 'f you kill hogs on the full they won't shrink. But, however, says I, bein's the moon's so fur off, I'm pesky afeard she wont keep the pork from shrinking But, John, there's one thing I do know, says I, and that is, if we scald him at just high tide, he wont lose an ounce by skrinkin'. Yes, says John, I know this to be true, for I've often seen it tried. Well, says I, I tell you what I'll do, John; I'll let my sister—you know my sister, Widder Small, fellow-citizens, what keeps house for me—I'll let her take the almanac, an' watch the clock, an' when it's just high water, she'll sing out, an' we'll stick and souse the critter. So, to suit me, Sister Small stuck a mark in our almanac—your old Robert B.'s—where it told the high tide, an' took her station at the door. Well, when 'twas about high tide, John and I lugged out the water to the tub, an' caught the hog. Pretty soon Sister Small sings out "High tide!" 'Pon that I stuck him with a butcher-knife and he bled like a serpent. In with him, says I. We then give him a rousin' scaldin' an' dressed an' weighed him. Well, next day I weighed him agin, an', dear me! don't you think, *he'd shrunk ten pounds and a half!* Something's to pay, says I. Into the house I hurried, and says I, Sister, get me the almanac, and let me see where you found, where't tells high water. The almanac was got I looked into it where she'd put a mark, an' as true's my name is Simon Vilderblows, if she hadn't made a mistake an' got a last year's one! This explains it all, says I, and I've lost jest ten and a half pounds of nice, sweet pork by sister's not been keerful 'bout lookin' at the date. The schoolmaster happening along I told him my misfortins, an' he only smiled and said 'twas done by evaporation. I told him he had better stick to his *Albrega,* an' not talk of what he did'nt know nothing about. My friends, I've nothing more to say. I feel that we are in a good cause, an' desarve success.

POLLY SIMPSON [*rising*].—I should be pleased to hear something from our president. Sister Snarl, can't you say something for the good of the cause?

GRANNY SNARL.—Men folks, women folks, an' feller-citizens, greetin! [*She stops and blows her nose with a ragged red pocket-handkerchief when the boys roar aloud.*] Stop yer larfin' up there'n the back seat! Ye ain't but little better than heathen! Wont some one that's a friend to woman's rights go an' larn them tarnups what manners is, an' stop their disturbin' this meetin'?

SIMON VILDERBLOWS.—I hope you boys will be civil there on the back seat.

GRANNY SNARL.—Feller-citizens, I would like to say a good deal, but you see I've got a terrible cold [*she coughs*]; got it a killin' my hog, which, by the way, was a buster, for he weighed two hundred and thirty pounds arter he's dressed and his liver taken out. Hogs like that are skerse in these diggins, you'd better believe [*the boys laugh*]. There now! it's jest as Sister Simpson has often said, the risin' gineration is an awful set of bein's. They don't know a mite better than to come to sech a solemn an' interestin' meetin' as this an' laif, an haw haw, an' hee hee, jests if 'twas a circus, panorandle, or nigger concert. I've been afeared all along that if we wimmen folks didn't take the reins in our own hands there'd be war an' bloodshed an' every thing else that's bad. And jest what I'se afeard on has come to pass; we've got inter trouble with our mother country, an' dear only knows when 'twill eend. I haint had a good dish o' Young Hyson this six months; an' what's more, I never shall, unless we wimmen folks rise rite up an' let em know who's who and what's what. Then, as Sister Simpson, an' Sister Lawrence, and Brother Vilderblows have jest said, coffee's riz, sweetening's riz, an' every thing else we have to buy has riz accordingly; and, fellow-citizens, they'll keep goin' up, till bimeby we shall be on the town, and then who'll take keer o' the poor? And what's to be done? methinks I hear ye all ax. I'll tell ye what's to be done. Let the wimmen take charge on the government, put in some good lady, like Sister Simpson, here, for Town Clark, an' sech wimmen as Sister Lawrence for Seleckmen and then if the men folks wants any of the small offices, sech as hog-reef or surveyor, why, we'll let 'em have 'em provided they'll swear to support the constitution of the United States. Do this, and you'll see how quick sugar, molasses, and other West Injee goods would come down! I shan't ask for any office myself, 'cause I haint got much of a school edication, and I don't want to take sech responsibility on my poor shoulders: but then ye know my vote'll tell Now, something has got to be done right a way—the sooner the better, Sister Simpson an' myself have talked the matter over and made up our minds to do something.

Boy.—The President will pardon my interruption, I rise to move that a contribution be taken up to defray the expenses of this meeting.

Another Boy.—I second the motion.

Granny Snarl.—Yer real kind, ye be! We'll now take a vote. All who's in favor of passin' round the hat to git money to pay for firewood, lights, an' sech like, will please say aye.

All.—Aye! aye!

Granny Snarl.—'Tis a vote, sartin's the world. The gentleman who's so kind as to think of payin' expenses, will he please carry round the hat, while Sister Simpson reads that little ditty she's writ for the occasion! [*Boy takes round the hat.*] Sister Simpson will now deliver the ditty. It's proper nice I kin tell ye, I've heard it once.

Polly Simpson [*reads in a loud, sharp voice*]

ODE IN BEHALF OF WIMMENS RIGHTS.

The men are real obstropolus,
  They wont mind their own biz-
Iness, and that's the reason why
  That tea and lasses both has riz:
And every thing that we do eat,
  And every thing that we do wear,
Have got to be so awful high—
  What shall we do, I do declare!

Molasses once was four and six;
  But now two dollars we must give;
And liquor, too, is such a price
  That tavern-keepers scarce can live;
And when last Sunday I'se at church,
  I heard Parson Jenkins in his
Sermon say, that flour and corn,
  And every kind of thing has riz.

Now don't you see the reason is
  The men are so obstropolus—
They will not let the wimmen vote,
  And things is growing worse and worse.

Now, we must rise and let 'em know
  What our rights be : and *then, I guess,*
That all kinds of West Ingee goods
  In prices will grow less and less !

Now we have all met here to-night—
  Sisters Lawrence, Snarl and I,
And Mr. Vilderblows, and all
  The rest of us—to see and try
To lay some plan to ease our lot
  And make things cheap, and **make a law,**
Whereby all fighting shall be stopped,
  And never have another war.

Now every woman that does live
  In any part of Greensboro,'
Must rise on next town meeting day,
  And to the ballot-box must go :
And then must vote—and then, I guess,
  Once more will have a good, brisk bis-
Iness, and shall no longer hear,
  That every kind of thing has riz.

[*The boy who carried round the hat, now deposits its contents on the desk (contents being a promiscuous mixture of buttons, nails, chips, and just five large coppers), and says to the President :*]

Boy.—The amount of money is not so great as I hoped to get, but still there's sufficient to pay the ex pense of oil and candles. And here let me say, I feel assured, that when the community shall awaken to a full sense of the importance of the glorious cause in which you, our honored President, and your patriotic colleagues, have so nobly engaged, they will rally around your bright banner, and put forward this great work toward its final consummation. That your praiseworthy and disinterested efforts may be crowned with ultimate success, is the heartfelt hope of your humble servant.— [*Bowing, retires.*]

Granny Snarl.—Bless ye! you're a noble-hearted creetur ! [*Putting the money in her pocket, and with her hand sweeping the buttons, etc., off the desk.*] If all the men-folks was sich as you be, there'd be no need of us wimmen-folks takin' matters in hand.

Polly Simpson.—The President had better put the funds in the hands of the collector, and let him settle the bills. He has already proved himself an honest and patriotic soul. Let him be our treasurer, by all means.

GRANNY SNARL.—Oh, I kin take keer on the funds myself.

POLLY SIMPSON.—But 'twould be better to do as I have suggested.

GRANNY SNARL.—I tell ye I kin take keer of it myself.

POLLY SIMPSON.—I know you'd take care of it, and in such a way as wouldn't benefit the society.

GRANNY SNARL.—What's that! D'ye think I'm inclined to cheat the public? [*Granny shakes her fist.*]

POLLY SIMPSON.—I haint said it.

GRANNY SNARL.—Well, ye mean it, if ye haint said it.

POLLY SIMPSON.—Yes, madam, I do mean it, and say it, too. I wouldn't trust you any further than I can see you. I've heard, 'fore now, of people's stealin' lard and flax; but I wont call names, for that aint my natur.

GRANNY SNARL.—Yer a miserable, low-lived, sharp-nosed, old scamp! You not only want wimmen's rights in gineral, but ye mean to take away my rights, too. Accuse me of stealin' right afore folks, do ye? I'll fix ye, you old Satin, one o' these days!

NANCY LAWRENCE.—I call the house to order!

GRANNY SNARL.—Better call that old pirate to order!

POLLY SIMPSON.—I call the president to order!

GRANNY SNARL.—Call me to order, hey? Now comes the time for reckonin' old lady! [*springing toward Polly.*]

ALL.—Order! order! order!

ALL.—Adjourn! adjourn! adjourn!

THE ORPHAN'S TRUST.

SCENE.—*A gipsy camp in the background. A young girl discovered in the act of withdrawing her hand from that of the Gipsy Queen.*

GIPSY.—

Not care to know your future, blue-eyed maiden?
Who *loves* you, *whom you love*, and whom shall *wed*?
What laces, satins, jewels, he will give you;
What acres, palaces and rentals, *leave* you;

How rich must be her thoughts, how treasure-laden;
To crowd such common hopes and dreams from that young
  golden head!

MAIDEN.—

Ah! gipsey, but I love! I love, dark sister!
The hand I worship robed this earth with bloom:
His glory clothes each far off, wandering planet;
Yet loving eyes in tiniest flowers may scan it,
And, with sweet fervency of heart, adore!
Thus my sweeet mother taught me; living, dying:
And, passing hence, so wide she left the door
Of that fair upper world, I scarce have missed her,
Or grieved her 'midst the songs of Heaven with crying:
So smiles Our Father's grace, e'en on the darksome tomb!

GIPSY.—

Thrice happy maid! my love is all unneeded,
Where faith and love like thine, assure the heart!
Yet deem by sooth, for common human feelings,
Your starry gems have true and bright revealings,
And, though full oft, through idle scorn unheeded,
The voice of God and fate, speaks through my mystic art!